The Income Investor

The Income Investor

Choosing Investments that Pay Cash Today and Tomorrow

Donald R. Nichols

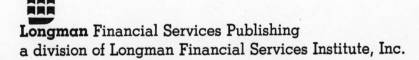

Longman Financial Services Publishing
a division of Longman Financial Services Institute, Inc.

While a great deal of care has been taken to provide accurate and current information, the ideas, suggestions, general principles and conclusions presented in this book are subject to local, state and federal laws and regulations, court cases and any revisions of same. The reader is thus urged to consult legal counsel regarding any points of law — this publication should not be used as a substitute for competent legal advice.

Executive Editor: Kathleen A. Welton
Project Editor: Roseann P. Costello
Copy Editor: Eugene Zucker
Interior/Cover Design: Edwin Harris

Published by Longman Financial Services Publishing
a division of Longman Financial Services Institute, Inc.

Printed in the United States of America.

89 90 10 9 8 7 6 5 4 3 2

Library of Congress Cataloging-in-Publication Data
Nichols, Donald R., 1948–
    The income investor.

    Includes index.
    1. Investments. I. Title.
HG4521.N47   1988   332.6'78   88-6838
ISBN 0-88462-738-1

During the past 20 years, everyone has been talking about and writing about capital growth, yet overwhelmingly people have been buying income investments. It's time for income investing to be recognized for what it is: a total investment strategy. This book is dedicated to every investor who recognizes the importance of income investments, and it carries special thanks to all of my clients who have shown me new ways to make income investments more useful for everyone.

Don Nichols

Contents

Reinvestment Risk and Opportunity. Strategies with Yields–Total Accumulations at Maturity. Serialized Maturities for Future Income. Yields and Maturities—Tax Deferred Accounts. Municipal Zeros as an Adjunct to IRAs and SERPs. Savings Bonds. Tutorial: Reading Price Quotations. Summary.

CHAPTER 7 Common and Preferred Stocks   69

Advantages and Disadvantages of Income Stocks. Dividends and Dividend Policy. The Dividend Announcement. Identifying Potential Income Stocks. Evaluating an Income Stock. Managing Income Stocks—Monitoring and Selling. Preferred Stocks. Tutorial: Reading Stock Quotations: *Using Quotations to Assess Dividend Yield.* Summary.

CHAPTER 8 Mutual Funds   81

Funds Specifically for Income Investors. Growth Funds for Income Investors. Quality and Maturity of Bond Funds. Net Asset Value—A Different Kind of Price. Investing in Mutual Funds. Managing Mutual Funds—Switch Privileges. Summary.

CHAPTER 9 Tax-Deferred Investments: Annuities, Employee Investment Plans, Individual Retirement Accounts   91

Basics of Annuities: *The Personal Annuity. Guaranteed Return Plans. Annuities plus Insurance.* Employee Investment Plans: *The Income Investor and EIPs. Managing EIPs. Should You Contribute to an EIP?* Individual Retirement Accounts: *Self-Employed Retirement Plans (SERPs). Managing Your IRA—Self-Directed Accounts and Mutual Funds. IRAs and the Income Investor. General Guidance for Income Investors and IRAs. Should You Contribute to an IRA? Can You Deduct IRA Contributions?* Comparing Tax-Deferred Investments: *Size of Contributions. Diversity and Control. Greatest Potential Accumulations.* Summary.

**CHAPTER 10 Options, International Securities,
                and Precious Metals   109**

Publicly Listed Call Options: *Features of Calls. Determinants of
Premium. The Income Investor—Writing Calls. Further Uses for
Calls.* Income from Foreign Investments: *Income from Foreign
Stocks and Bonds. Income from Foreign Annuities.* Precious
Metals as an Income Investment. Summary.

**SECTION III
The Professional Income Investor   119**

**CHAPTER 11 The Yield Curve and Term Structure
                of Interest Rates   121**

Constructing the Term-Yield Graph. Identical Maturities—
Assessing Quality and Yield. Assessing Liquidity, Market Risk,
and Reinvestment Risk. Assessing the Greatest Yield—Quality
Constant, Market Risk Indifferent. Assessing the Greatest
Yield—Quality Trade-Offs, Maturity Constant. Constant Dollar
Securities—Quality, Market Risk, Yield. Comparing Investments
of Higher Yield. Comparison with Stocks. Term-Yield and
Decisions to Sell or Consume. Yield that Seems Too Good To Be
True. Summary.

CHAPTER 12 Income Investments and Inflation   133

Defining Inflation—Consumption *and* Investment. Inflationary
cycles—Onset, Maturity, and Decline: *Income Investments for the
Onset of Inflation. Income Investments for Fully Confirmed
Inflation. Income Investments for Declining Inflation.* Inflation and
Trading Patterns for Income Investors. Income Stocks and
Lower-Rated Bonds as Inflationary Investments. Summary.

CHAPTER 13 Income Investments for Hard
                    Times—Recession and Depression   145

The Indicators of Recession. Income Investments and
Recession—Sector Analysis. Beyond Sector Analysis—Inflationary
Recessions: *Responding to Government Actions during Inflationary
Recession.* Deflationary Recessions: *Deflationary
Recessions—Sector Analysis and Term-Yield.* Genuine Economic
Depression: *Depression and Income Investors. Select Treasury
Securities for Depression. Term-Yield and Depression. Income
Investments and "the Devil's Profits".* Summary.

CHAPTER 14 The Aggressive or Transient
                    Income Investor   163

The Transient Income Investor. The Aggressive Income Investor.
Reinvestment Risk and Quality. Term-Yield and Aggressive or
Transient Income Investors. What Confirmed Income Investors
Owe Other Income Investors. Confirmed Income Investors and
Bond Swaps. Summary.

CHAPTER 15 The Retired Income Investor   173

Immediate Retirement Income—Social Security, EIPs, Personal
Annuities. Converting Your IRA to Current Income. Investment
Income Outside the IRA. Serializing Zeros for Current Income.
Addressing Growth with Income Investments. Summary.

SECTION IV
The Efficient Corner Portfolio   181

Variance and Return in the Efficient Portfolio. Offsetting
Characteristics Improve Stability. Offsetting Characteristics
Improve Returns. Return for Variance; Variance for Return. The
Efficient Frontier Portfolio. Personal Portfolio Preferences. The
Efficient Corner Portfolio. Shifting Frontiers. Initial Portfolios and

Introduction

Over good times, bad times, inflation, recession, depression, and the varying times of their lives, American investors have wisely favored investments that make cash payments, especially investments that pay interest and dividends. The term that accurately and comprehensively describes these investments is *income investments,* and the term that describes people who own them is *income investors.* Without doubt, you are an income investor.

Your first investment was more than likely a savings account or a U.S. savings bond. These investments produce income—current interest in the case of the savings account, accreted interest in the case of the savings bond. Without knowing it, you started your financial life as an income investor, and, like millions of Americans, you are probably still an income investor.

If you own certificates of deposit, money market funds, or any kind of bond and bond mutual fund, the interest you receive classifies you as an income investor. If you own rental property, a stock mutual fund, or dividend-paying stocks, their dividends and royalties make you an income investor. If you participate in an annuity, an IRA, a retirement plan from a company or union, or an employee investment plan from your corporation, you are an income investor because current income from stocks and bonds is compounding federally untaxed on your behalf.

Income investments pay you while you own them, and you can use the payments for current expenses or for reinvested compounding and future income. Current income is a considerable reason to prefer income investments over capital growth investments that produce cash only when they're sold. However, there is more to commend income investments than income. Properly identified and chosen, individual income investments offer advantages that no other form of investment can match:

- *Capital stability*—important when other investments are fluctuating wildly in price.

- *Market-level interest*—important for investors who need maximum current payments and have little time for market watching.

- *Locked-in certainty of interest*—important for investors who require known payments and known payment schedules.

- *Highest quality*—important when investors face uncertain economies and business conditions.

- *Variations in quality*—important for investors who seek higher returns by accepting higher risks.

- *Extraordinary ranges of maturities*—important for investment planning whether you're planning through tomorrow morning or into the next century.

- *Differing payment schedules*—important for investors who stagger their income to meet life needs.

- *Liquidity*—an important consideration in responding to markets, economies, and opportunity, and the ability to convert investments into cash quickly is characteristic of most income investments.

- *Tax-favored returns*—important for investors in higher tax brackets, investors who need alternatives to tax-offset investments, and investors who are compounding interest and dividends for a future date

- *Extreme flexibility*, more so than has been acknowledged—important for investors who respond wisely to economic changes and evolving life needs.

Finally, one of the most important and overlooked features of income investments is their unparalleled innovation. Income investments have changed more in the past ten years than any other category of investment. Apart from plain vanilla stocks, bonds, and certificates of deposit, today's income investor can choose among variable rate corporate bonds, designer certificates of deposit, bonds with warrants, bonds in foreign currencies, quality bonds and junk bonds, zero coupon bonds that convert to conventional bonds, zero corporate bonds that convert to stocks, zero coupon certificates of deposit, bonds convertible into precious metals and special types of income enhancements to long-standing investments. Every one of these innovations creates a new attraction for income investments and a new category of income investor.

Income investments can serve you and promote portfolio profits in ways other securities cannot and in ways you may not have considered. There is virtually no personal circumstance, investment goal, or economic setting that income investments can't serve when you employ their full range of features. Income investments are important now, and their importance is growing. Consider the evidence:

The wall of worry for stocks grows higher. Investors are looking for alternatives to stocks, and income investments can produce predictable returns while conserving capital. They are the alternative to stocks that investors seek.

Investors are asking serious questions about the U.S. economy. Whether the present economic boom ends in recession, inflation, or depression, income investments can be tailored to economic hard times more successfully than other investments, and concerned economy-watchers are learning more about income investments.

Post-1986 tax laws eliminated deductions, damaged real limited partnerships, ruined IRAs for many Americans, altered advantages of Uniform Gifts to Minors Accounts, and taxed capital gains as current income. Income investments such as federally untaxed municipal bonds are replacing the advantages of these bygone investments. Moreover, The Internal Revenue Code of 1986—to say nothing of Congressional intentions to pursue its precedents—is most rewarding for investments that produce straightforward, visible income.

Following new restrictions on deductible investment in IRAs, 20 million Americans looked for new investments that provide untaxed or tax-deferred compounding for retirement. They found their "new" investments in municipal bonds, municipal bond funds, and zero coupon municipal bonds, all of which are income investments that pay federally untaxed compounding and federally untaxed current income before and during retirement. The retirement-minded are also indirect income investors substituting annuities and life insurance/investment programs that rely on income investments to compound untaxed.

An estimated five million investors can continue making tax-exempt investments in Individual Retirement Accounts. Income investments are ideal for tax-deferred accounts because their interest and dividends compound untaxed. Self Employed Retirement Plans profit more than ever from income investments. Not only do their interest and dividends compound tax deferred, but investments are also deductible from income.

More than ever, demographics are creating income investors. Today workers retire in their 50s and live into their 80s—a 30-year period, which suggests that baby boomers will overlap their parents as retirees. Income investments are central to planning for retirement and for income in the retirement portfolio.

The evidence is compelling. Markets, the economy, changed tax laws, and population demographics suggest that income investments are the appropriate investments for our time. They also suggest that you learn more about income investing for these reasons and because income investments can meet your life and investment situations.

Highly taxed investors can concentrate on municipal bonds and municipal bond funds, which pay interest exempt from federal income taxation—and in some cases from state and local income taxation.

Investors seeking tax-deferred returns can draw upon income investments for compounding now and spendable income later. Investors who want to supplement a retirement-anticipation portfolio or to make provision for children's tuition find that income investments are the key.

Investors who want cash-in-hand receipts to supplement retirement income can select from among scores of income investments that are bidding to join their portfolios.

Investors wanting the bluest-chip conservative investments can select investment-grade corporate and government bonds that offer high returns and security of principal. Aggressive investors may choose lower-rated bonds and high-dividend stocks to match their high-flying temperaments.

The internationally minded investor who wants to diversify beyond American shores or to add the possible boost of currency translations to a portfolio knows that international income funds and foreign bonds and certificates of deposit are perfect for these purposes.

Not only do broad conditions favor income investments, but all individual types of investors are served personally by such investments. Now consider yourself and the situations you face.

Maybe you're one or several of the types of investors described above and you want to know what income investments can do for you. Maybe the economy, changed tax laws, and your life situation don't fit the portfolio you now have. Maybe you aren't happy with the way your portfolio has performed and you want ease and understandability of income investments. If so, you're ready to become an income investor or, if you already are one, to become a more successful income investor.

The four sections into which *The Income Investor* is divided prepare you to become a competent and comprehensive income investor.

Section I is an overview of investing and income investing. It explains fundamentals of capital and investing, acquaints you with risks and returns of investing, introduces basic principles of income investments—maturity, types of yields, compounding, capital stability—and tutors you in lasting basics for your life as an income investor.

Section II provides exhaustive coverage of each type of income investment, ranging from the familiar certificate of deposit through stocks and bonds, tax-deferred income investments for IRAs and SERPs, the singular uses of zero coupon investments, annuity-insurance investments, and even such special types of income investments as international securities and stock options. In chapters singling out each type of income investment, Section II itemizes risks and rewards, advantages and disadvantages, the origin and recognition of differing yields, and assessment of the quality of income. Tutorials to selected chapters refresh your understanding of how to read market quotations.

Section III elevates you to the level of the professional, first by teaching you to employ the term-yield graph to compare income investments. With your knowledge of term-yield, Sections I and II become fully functional information for continuing investment decisions. Inflation is always said to make income investments worthless. Section III shows why this is not true and how to structure income investments for inflation. Economic recession challenges income investments, but Section III reveals how to understand and respond to that challenge. Genuine economic depression is devastating for an economy, but not necessarily for income investors. Retired investors are always concerned with income investments, and Section III teaches them how to invest astutely. It discusses techniques for investors who accept more risk for the possibility of more reward and transitory income investors who use income investments as a parking lot for capital awaiting other types of investments. It also shows what other income investors can learn from such investors.

Section IV brings you to the most central aspect of sustained income investing—creating an efficient frontier portfolio that mixes and matches income investments according to the risks and returns you select on the basis of the knowledge you've acquired.

Just as income investments are indispensable to your financial planning, *The Income Investor* can be indispensable to your financial bookshelf. With intelligence, understanding, and study, you can make income investments permanently rewarding for your life and portfolio.

SECTION

I

Overview of Income Investing

1

Capital, Risks, and Rewards

There are only two decisions about money: save it or spend it. If you set aside a portion of savings or defer consumption in a particular way, namely investment, there are again only two consequences: increased saving or increased consumption. The ultimate end of investment is consumption. There is no avoiding this fact. If you do not consume your investment returns, your government or heirs will. Therefore, investment capital is *money that stands between saving and consumption and could be used to increase either.* But investment capital has a further distinction: its increase comes only from accepting risk.

RISKS OF INVESTING

Banks and S&Ls tell depositors that their savings accounts or certificates of deposit are "risk free." The same is heard about U.S. Treasury notes and bonds. Money market funds are sometimes billed as "riskless." These representations are wrong. Every investment requires risk. Investment capital is at risk because there is no risk-free

3

investment. Understanding this, we understand another aspect of investment capital: it grows only because investors accept the form of risk it entails. When most of us speak of risk, we mean "losing capital I invested." In investing, risk of capital loss is only one type of risk—market risk.

Market risk refers to circumstances that diminish the absolute value of capital, and one source of market risk is that associated with income investments traded on public markets. On October 19, 1987, the Dow Jones Industrial Average caved in by over 500 points, accompanied by similar free-fall in other market averages. Hallowed IBM lost 46 points. We can generally agree that nothing in the economy, in corporate profits, or in IBM was much different on October 19 than on October 18. The market created this disaster on this day for some reason, and investors participated in the disaster as a consequence of the inherent market risk associated with publicly listed securities.

Business risk is associated with earnings because they are the source of capital gains and all investment income. If you own a stock or bond, business risk can produce losses because lackluster earnings are expressed in the prices of securities traded on public markets.

Default risk refers to two events: the possibility an investment will pay no return because its issuer is out of business and the possibility an investment will pay less than expected returns because business has been awful. Commonly associated with debtor-creditor investments, default risk may also apply to owner-equity investments through the decrease or omission of dividends.

Market risk, business risk, and default risk apply to income investments because some income investments are traded on public markets, because issuers of securities must produce revenues with which to pay interest and dividends, and because every income payment is vulnerable to default or reduction by the issuer.

Economic risk results from macroeconomic influences such as interest rates, unemployment, business earnings, and the balance of payments. When the macroeconomy turns down, earnings unavoidably suffer, presenting business risk and default risk that are reflected in market prices.

Inflation is a sustained increase in the general level of prices. The ultimate end of all investment is consumption, and an increase in prices makes consumption more attractive unless investment can produce returns in excess of both inflation and deferred consumption. Because many income investments pay a fiat rate that doesn't account for inflation, fixed income investments don't retain their purchasing power. They are vulnerable to **inflation risk** unless they are managed wisely.

Interest rate risk is the relationship between the interest paid by a particular investment and the overall interest rates available in the economy. Economy-wide interest rates change, rising and falling, but interest on income investments seldom changes, because interest payments are fixed by covenant. Accordingly, economy-wide changes in interest rates cause fixed income investments to fall in price when interest rates rise and to rise in price when interest rates fall. In short, interest rate risk causes capital fluctuation and potential capital losses.

From the income investor's perspective, a potent aspect of interest rate risk is **reinvestment risk**—opportunity, or lack of it, to retain a constant yield on income investments. To illustrate:

Interest rates in the economy rise. If you hold fixed income investments, such as most bonds, the interest they receive does not increase. Then, not only do the prices of your old, publicly traded income investments fall, but you lose income because your old investments do not provide the higher returns of a higher-interest environment.

Second, economy-wide interest rates fall. Although publicly traded fixed income investments will then increase in price, falling interest rates on such investments represent a loss to investors. Let's say you bought a bond when the prevailing interest rate was ten percent. When the bond matures, the prevailing interest rate is six percent. You've lost four percent because you can't reinvest at the previously higher rate.

Thus, reinvestment risk is a double-edged sword, as we will see repeatedly.

Economic risk, inflation risk, interest rate risk, and reinvestment risk are key risks for income investors. The earlier trio of risks—

market, business, and default—can be managed more successfully because income investors can select income investments that are less vulnerable or invulnerable to those three risks. Economic, inflation, interest rate, and reinvestment risk will be forever prevalent in the income component of the portfolio. These four risks can be reduced substantially, but no income investment is invulnerable to them.

Changes in tax laws—**tax rate risk**—are vicious because they can make today's smart investment unwise in the future.

Examples are numerous. Congress changed the taxation of capital gains many times before making them taxable as current income. The first $100 or $200 of dividend income used to be excluded from tax. Individual Retirement Accounts were at first available to a few workers, then to all workers (with deductibility of contributions and tax-deferred compounding), and now to all workers but not necessarily with deductibility of contributions. Some types of municipal bonds that had been encouraged by tax laws were almost eradicated in 1986.

Tax rate risk is part of **political risk**, which is another nation's disposition toward business, foreigners, international trade, foreign expansionism—basically toward anything, including revolutions, political overthrow, and invasion by other nations. Political risk overlaps all economic and market risk. Inflation in Israel makes Israeli bonds unattractive; devaluations ruined high-interest savings accounts in Mexico; property taxes are so complex in France that only sophisticated property masters and tax mavens invest there; the courts of Islamic nations do not recognize interest as a lender's entitlement, making bonds of those nations and their corporations suspect; Americans used to earn nice returns from bonds of Cuba, Russia, and Poland—used to. When you expatriate income investments, you increase the political risk in your portfolio.

POSITIVE ASPECTS OF RISK FOR INCOME INVESTORS

One overwhelmingly positive aspect of all risks is that without risk there would be no reward. Investment risks produce investment rewards. That's why investors undertake these risks. For income investors, another positive aspect of investment risks is that diversity of income investments permits income investors to choose and manage these risks more carefully than do other investors.

The income investor who is concerned about the risks of public markets can choose constant dollar income investments, such as money market funds, savings accounts, certificates of deposit, and savings bonds.

The income investor concerned with business risk and default risk can select Treasury securities or certificates of deposit—if FDIC or FSLIC is involved.

The income investor who is concerned with income tax risk can choose municipal bonds, which are exempt from federal and sometimes state income taxes, or Treasury securities, which are exempt from state income taxes.

Income investors keep income investments in the United States to reduce political risk to that of a nation they know.

Income investors manage economic, interest rate, inflation, and reinvestment risk though income investments with reduced vulnerability to them. Treasury securities minimize the results of economic risk. Money market funds minimize interest rate risk and inflation risk. Interest rate risk and reinvestment risk can be reduced by attention to maturities.

SUMMARY

Chapter 1 has shown that all investments entail risk, income investments included. Many types of income investments are more vulnerable to some types of risk than to others, yet many are more invulnerable to certain risks than are other types of investments. By understanding income investments, we can expose ourselves to positive aspects of risk and avoid negative aspects of risks that we don't want to accept. Your confidence in income investments can be high because they can be managed to avoid some risks and reduce others—and with greater reliability of result than is obtained from other types of investments.

2

Origins and Issues of Income Investments: Price, Maturity, Income, Yield, Quality, Liquidity

Now we focus specifically on income investments. We will examine how *initial* issues of stocks and bonds are priced, how dividends and interest are established, how maturity is determined, and how quality and maturity influence the price and payment of income investments. Once stocks and bonds enter *public* trading, all of these determinants are factored into the market price, not the issue price.

These determinants of income investments present special considerations in managing income investments for investors who purchase them at original issue and in public markets. Those considerations include capital stability, reinvestment opportunity, liquidity, and, in particular, yield—yield not only for income investors who need cash payments but also for income investors who can permit income investments to compound for continuing growth.

PRICE OF INCOME INVESTMENTS

When a new issue of any publicly traded security is brought to market, the price of that issue is established through the advice of investment bankers. With stocks, determining the issue price is a complex matter that takes into account the prospects for the company's profitability, the receptiveness of the market to new issues, and considerations that may be more emotional than analytic.

The situation is less complex with regard to the issue price of bonds. The price of newly issued bonds is nearly always par value— $1,000. Sometimes an investment banker will counsel the corporation to issue a new bond at slightly below par, but not too much below par. Therefore, the price of a newly issued corporate bond is a matter of investment tradition: bonds come in par values of $1,000. At initial issue, Treasury and municipal bonds present much the same situation. Their price is nearly always par or close to par because American bonds are born with a par value of $1,000.

After a stock or bond enters public trading, its price is determined by the "market"—that is, by other investors' assessment of whether ownership of the stock or bond is desirable. Once weaned from its investment banker, the security is at the mercy of the market.

When most bonds enter trading in public markets, their coupon rate is fixed, as are their other features, such as maturity. Their price will then rise and fall to reflect the attractiveness of their fixed features in comparison to the features of other securities and to the economy-wide rate of interest. This is why capital gains and losses are possible with publicly traded bonds.

Fiat prices are set for untraded securities such as certificates of deposit and savings bonds. Most certificates of deposit are available in amounts of $500 to $1 million. The banking system picked those prices. The Treasury, too, has fiat-priced debt. Savings bonds are priced at half of par.

QUALITY IN INCOME INVESTING

"Quality" refers to the likelihood of receiving timely returns and punctual repayment of the principal. Investments that present absolute to strong likelihood of paying timely interest and repaying the principal punctually are *investment grade*. Bonds achieve investment-grade status through review by rating agencies. These independent bodies pore over statistics reflecting an issuer's ability to service indebtedness and announce their decisions with ratings ranging from AAA ("triple-A") to D (in default).

Investments rated AAA, AA, A, and BBB are investment grade. They represent absolute to very strong likelihood that investors won't get stiffed on interest and principal. Treasury debt is rated AAA. Debt rated BB, B, and CCC offers more risk of default. These are the junk bonds that aggressive income investors seek and to which we will refer again in Section III. Debt rated CC and C is clearly speculative, with open questions about the solvency of the issuer. Debt rated D has already defaulted on an interest or principal payment.

The ultimate in quality is U.S. Treasury securities. Second are certificates of deposit from depositories belonging to the FDIC and the FSLIC. A close third are blue-chip corporate bonds. Agency ratings on corporate stocks—those few that are rated—are less pertinent than agency ratings on corporate bonds. However, a high rating on a corporate bond does, in some respects, transfer to the stock of the rated corporation.

Assessments of quality change as bonds enter public trading— Treasuries excepted. With corporate bonds, quality may deteriorate with business conditions. With municipals, quality may deteriorate with a municipality's tax base. Rating agencies reflect such changes, positive and negative, with revisions in ratings.

MATURITY OF INCOME INVESTMENTS

Stocks don't mature—though some can be called back from the market. Corporations are presumed to be in business indefinitely, and their stock is presumed to be forever outstanding.

Like the coupon rate, maturity is specified by the covenant of a bond issue. Whether a corporation decides to go short term, intermediate term, or long term depends on why it raises money by issuing bonds. Typically, a bond issue that capitalizes or refinances a corporation has a longer maturity, giving the issuer latitude in getting on its financial feet. An established corporation will often issue shorter-term bonds to finance a particular project, revenues from which support the lower coupon rate, pay the principal, and leave the project's income for shareholders.

The Treasury raises bonds for many reasons—to finance the country, to repay maturing Treasury debt, to bridge a gap between current expenses and future tax revenues. Accordingly, Treasury debt comes in maturities ranging from 30 days to 30 years.

Municipal debt is another story. Municipal investors are skittish and like shorter maturities. Municipalities like longer debt. So both parties compromise on intermediate-term debt, which is how most general obligation municipal indebtedness achieves its initial maturity.

When a bond is initially issued, its maturity correlates with every other aspect of the bond—its quality and coupon, its price, attractiveness in comparison with that of other investments, its overall desirability.

Once a bond enters public trading, its maturity again correlates with its other fixed features in such management issues as capital fluctuation, reinvestment risk, market price, and yield. This is so because the longer bonds are present in public markets, the more closely they approach maturity. A long-term bond that was initially issued to mature in 20 years is a different bond when it is a year from maturity.

LIQUIDITY IN INCOME INVESTING

Liquidity is the ability to convert your income investment into cash. Investments traded on public markets are obviously liquid, for they can be bought and sold as you require. Unlisted investments such as certificates are not liquid.

Liquidity is your response to opportunity and uncertainty— opportunity, because cash is the most liquid asset and you can do anything with it; uncertainty, because investors "go to cash" when economic risk, market risk, and default risk discourage investment. Liquidity is important if you want to get out of a losing investment (preserve capital stability) or to reinvest in a new income opportunity (reduce exposure to interest rate risk). With the exception of certificates and savings bonds, income investments are highly liquid.

DETERMINANTS OF INVESTMENT INCOME— DIVIDENDS AND INTEREST

Except for the stocks of public utilities, most new issues of stocks are not brought to market with an established dividend. First, the stock and the company issuing it must earn the revenues that produce dividends.

Once a stock and the corporation it represents have been seasoned by investment markets and business operations, dividends are the consequence of the corporation's dividend policy with respect to earnings. Corporations may pay out a percentage of their earnings as dividends and may also base dividends on those paid by competing companies in their industry. Thus, dividends are initially set and subsequently raised or lowered according to profitability, the target percentage of earnings paid in dividends, and the dividends paid by rival competitors for capital.

A corporation issuing a new bond will offer a rate of interest that is based on the solvency of the corporation, that is competitive with the economy and rival firms, and that increases with the bond's maturity. These factors are expressed in the coupon payment of the bond—actual cash disbursement to investors.

Treasury bonds set coupon payments based on the requirements of the market when these bonds are issued. If the market requires a $70 coupon or a $100 coupon, the Treasury affixes that coupon to its bonds when they are issued. The immediacy of funding requirements and attention to the market rates of the moment are reasons why Treasury bonds of similar maturities carry widely varying coupons.

Municipal bonds typically base their coupon payments on a differential from the coupon payments of Treasury bonds.

Institutions fix the interest of untraded interest-bearing securities, such as most certificates of deposit, according to the rates offered by competing institutions in their area. To some extent, the rates paid on certificates of deposit have been becoming national since the advent of bank deregulation. Issuing banks or S&Ls figure the rate they have to pay and offer that rate, which typically changes from week to week.

The interest rates of a savings account with an S&L or a share account with a credit union are fiat rates. For reasons known only to themselves, S&Ls have picked $5^1/2$ percent as their rate of interest.

A money market fund is a true market rate, although a select rate—the rate on short-term investments. A money market fund promises nothing except to find the best rates presented by short-term investments.

REVIEW OF RELATIONSHIPS

Before advancing, let's review the interaction of price, quality, maturity, liquidity, and income.

The price of a newly issued stock or bond is determined by the counsel of investment bankers and by a tradition that has established a par of $1,000 for bonds. A fiat price applies to untraded securities, such as certificates of deposit and savings bonds. Once a security enters trading, its price is determined by the market's assessment. The price of untraded securities is either constant or determined in private markets maintained by the issuer.

At initial issue and during trading, the quality of a bond is judged by knowledgeable rating agencies.

At initial issue, the maturity of a bond derives from the issuer's need for borrowed capital. In public markets, maturity is determined by the security's nearness to maturity; a 20-year bond or certificate becomes a 1-year bond or certificate 19 years after it has been issued.

Liquidity is achieved through public trading and through the approach of maturity.

Dividend and interest income is a factor in all these considerations for issuers of income securities because issuers induce investors to accept securities of differing price, quality, maturity, and liquidity through dividends and interest.

Income is a factor for investors, whether they are investing in originally issued or long-traded securities, because income is their inducement to select securities of differing price, quality, maturity, and liquidity. We will return to this point throughout *The Income Investor*.

YIELD

Yield is the percentage relationship that return bears to investment, and it is the concept that draws together payments, price, quality, and maturity. Yield is not merely the amount of interest, dividends, or other payments; it is the relationship of amount invested to amount of income earned. Different income investments offer different types of yields; yield changes if income is reinvested, and yield changes whether you buy a security when it is initially issued or on the public exchange. The following yields (covered under appropriate investments in Section II) are important to income investors:

Dividend yield: The dividend payment of a stock divided by the purchase price of the stock.

Coupon yield: The coupon payment of a bond divided by the par value of the bond.

Current yield: The coupon payment of a bond divided by the purchase price of the bond.

Accreted yield: The yield that accrues from the difference between the price paid for an investment and the par value received when the investment matures, as with savings bonds and zero coupon bonds. This type of yield looks like a capital gain, but it isn't.

Yield to maturity: The total yield that a bond provides from interest plus or minus changes in its price.

Nominal yield (also called "nominal interest"): The stated yield that savings accounts and certificates of deposit pay; somewhat like coupon yields for bonds.

Compound yield (also "compound interest" and "effective yield"): The yield that income investments pay by letting income grow; also, the return from reinvesting interest and dividends.

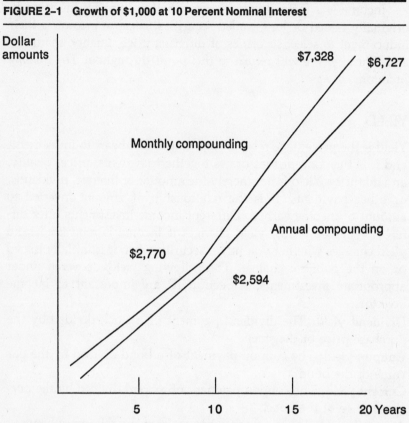

FIGURE 2–1   Growth of $1,000 at 10 Percent Nominal Interest

Dollar
amounts

Monthly compounding $7,328 $6,727

Annual compounding

$2,770

$2,594

5   10   15   20 Years

Tax-equivalent yield: A comparison of yields on fully taxable investments with yields on partially taxable or nontaxable investments; also used to examine tax-deferred investment yields.

In addition, yield is a function of time as well as a function of principal paid and income received. The yield of an investment that produces $1 in one year is different from the yield of an investment that produces $1 in ten years.

PRESENT INCOME AND COMPOUNDED INCOME

Income investments produce income, and income must ultimately be consumed. But the word is *ultimately*. Income investors have a

---

FIGURE 2–2   Growth of $1,000 at 5½ Percent, 7 Percent and 10 Percent

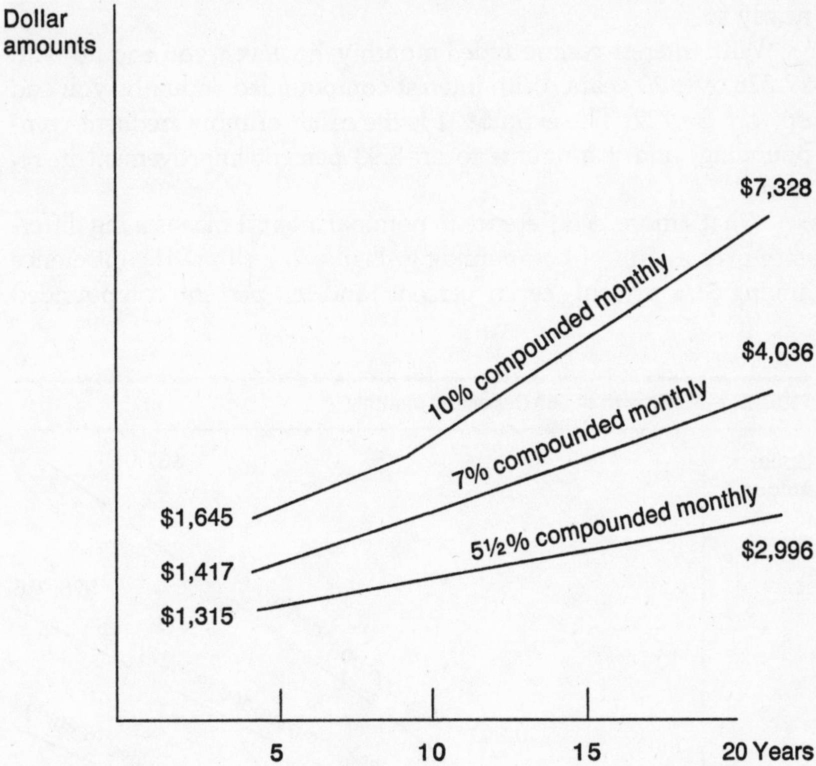

Dollar
amounts

$7,328

$4,036

10% compounded monthly

7% compounded monthly

$1,645

5½% compounded monthly

$2,996

$1,417

$1,315

5   10   15   20 Years

choice: they can select income investments because they need spendable income, as retirees often do, or they can reinvest for compounding—that is, for greater spendable income in the future. The ability to reinvest for future consumption brings investors to "the miracle of compounding." Although not miraculous, compounding is startling.

All investments pay a nominal yield—a flat, declared sum. But interest can compound to produce a greater sum if you don't spend it, because compounding results in the payment of interest on interest.

With compounding, the nominal interest rate becomes an effective interest rate. Figure 2–1 shows the growth of $1,000 at ten percent nominal interest for 20 years. The staggering item, first of all, is accumulated value. Over 20 years, your $1,000 grows sevenfold or nearly so.

With interest compounded monthly, however, you end up with $7,328 over 20 years. With interest compounded annually, you end up with $6,727. The extra $601 is the result of more frequent compounding, and it amounts to an 8.93 percent improvement in return.

What's more, a difference in nominal interest means a big difference over a term of compounding. Figure 2–2 shows the difference among 5¹/₂ percent, seven percent, and ten percent compounded

FIGURE 2–3   Growth of $50 Deposited Monthly

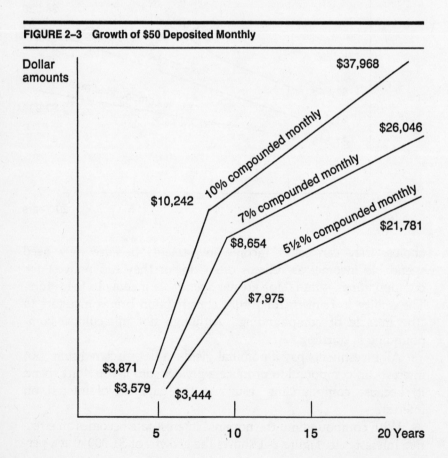

monthly over 20 years. Although accumulations are similar up to five years, compounding kicks in dramatically between ten and 20 years.

However, investing a single sum—as you do when buying a bond—is only one of the income investor's alternatives. Many income investors contribute regular amounts to their income portfolio. A series of deposits, even modest deposits contributed monthly to a money fund, can accumulate impressive sums. Figure 2–3 shows what happens to $50 monthly invested at 5$^{1/2}$ percent, seven percent, and 10 percent compounded monthly. Again, note that compounding produces modestly different returns up to five years. Between five to ten and ten to 20 years, however, the payment of interest on interest produces dramatic increases in compounded rates.

Some investments compound by themselves—money funds, depositary accounts, and mutual funds are prime sources of automatic compounding. However, many income investments involve a check in the mail—notably dividends and bond interest. If you want interest and dividend checks to compound, you have to reinvest them immediately, most likely in a money market fund.

SUMMARY

The lessons of Chapter 2 prepare us for issues that we confront more fully in Sections III and IV. But as we enter Section II and a discussion of specific income investments, we must understand that each of those investments presents not only singular features but also represents gradations in price, quality, maturity, income, yield, quality, and liquidity.

In the income component of the portfolio, those gradations present trade-offs in the matters we've discussed so far, because income investors must make active decisions regarding risk, reward, and features. We will see, for example, that bonds with longer maturities and lower quality typically offer higher coupon payments and yields. But longer maturities and lower quality mean less capital stability and greater default risk. We will see that untraded income investments offer great capital stability but that typically their yields are lower and they offer less liquidity. We will see that income investors must choose features and consequences knowing that their decisions are trade-offs serving their requirements for current or compounded returns, stability, growth, and satisfaction.

SECTION

The Types of Income Investments

With the basic principles of income investing behind us, we are ready to examine specific types of income securities. As we will see, each income investment provides a particular type of income and a particular set of characteristics to be considered. As always, each entails a risk and each provides a reward. Further, many income investments offer one or two special features that set them apart from other income investments. These special features often make the difference in our decisions to buy and sell them.

We start Section II with debtor-creditor investments, after which we move to owner-equity investments. Then we discuss tax-deferred income from some "exotic" alternatives that are available.

Debtor-creditor investments represent a borrower-lender relationship. With such investments, unlike owner-equity investments, you "own" nothing except the issuer's responsibility to pay you interest and repay your capital, but that responsibility is a binding one. D-Cs provide contractual returns. They entitle you to payment of only specified interest and only for a specified period, at the end of which they repay the principal (money market funds excepted).

Most debtor-creditor investments pay a fiat rate of interest because, unlike owner-equity investments, they have a covenant. However, some pay variable rates. A certificate of deposit maturing in five years will pay, say, eight percent. You get no less, but you get no more. D-Cs impose a specified holding period before you receive interest and principal. That period may be brief (a money market fund pays interest every day), or it may be lengthy and varied (some bonds may pay interest every six months but not repay the principal until the next century). D-C investments have a terminal value that is *usually* equivalent to your investment. If you buy a bond for $1,000, that bond won't be worth more than $1,000 when it matures.

Owner-equity investments differ in several ways from debtor-creditor investments, but as corporate stocks are the only owner-equity investment we will discuss, the differences will be clear when we arrive at Chapter Seven.

The point to remember is this: Income investors can choose owner-equity *and* debtor-creditor investments for income.

3

Certificates of Deposit

Type
Certificates of deposit
Savings accounts

Advantages
Capital stability
No fee and commission

Risk Avoided
Market risk

Income
Interest
Fully taxed
Compounded or current income

Disadvantages
Fiat interest*
Illiquidity

Risks Accepted
Inflation risk
Reinvestment risk

Among the most common and most frequently purchased income investments are certificates of deposit from banks, savings and loan associations, credit unions, and brokerages.

Certificates are contractual deposits. You agree to leave funds with an institution for a specified period, and the institution agrees to pay you a stated rate of interest plus compounding. At the end of that period, the institution returns the amount you initially invested plus interest. As a consequence of straightforward circumstances, these income investments have many attractions.

They are available without commissions and fees, and they are easily purchased from virtually any financial institution. They never vary in price. Their constant dollar price appeals to investors concerned about capital losses and market risk. They pay predictable interest that, depending on the size of your deposit, you can arrange to have mailed to you for current income or leave on deposit for compounding. Generally, only larger-denomination certificates offer a current income payment. Interest increases with the term of deposit, ranging from slightly more than a passbook rate for short certificates to interest akin to that of Treasury securities for longer maturities.

Certificates are available in maturities ranging from six months to 20 years and in investment amounts varying from $500 to $1 million, although a minimum investment of $1,000 is customary. They are available to income investors of all budgets and preferences in maturity.

Certificates are highly secure against default risk if the institution issuing them is affiliated with the Federal Deposit Insurance Corporation, the Federal Savings and Loan Insurance Corporation, or a related federal or state overseer. High quality makes certificates acceptable for conservative and quality-minded portfolios.

Chief among the drawbacks of certificates is their illiquidity. As a contractual deposit, certificates are "bound" for their agreed duration. If more attractive income opportunities arise and you cash your certificate prior to maturity to take advantage of them, you forfeit interest.

Most certificates pay fixed interest and compounding rates that are established on the date of issue. Therefore, they can be vulnerable to inflation risk. Interest from certificates is fully taxable by Uncle Sam and by state and local governments. Most certificates are "locked." You can invest $550 in a $500 certificate, but you cannot invest $500 and add $50 later.

NEW PRODUCTS

Depository institutions have created new products that counteract many of these disadvantages. The "designer certificate" permits investors to select a term of maturity and a rate of interest that are less rigid than those of the customary certificate. For example, where a normal certificate may pay eight percent for deposits of five years, investors can negotiate a designer certificate of four years that pays between seven and eight percent.

Investors who have recently taken a retirement distribution from an employer or union pension may have $100,000 for a jumbo certificate of deposit. Where guarantors are involved, the jumbo is secure against default and market fluctuations. Jumbos pay competitive rates that may be fixed or variable, thereby overcoming one disadvantage of certificates. Jumbos come in short and long maturities. Some can be sold anytime, overcoming the illiquidity of most certificates.

Variable rate certificates pay fluctuating interest whose rate is determined by the rate of inflation or by the interest rate on competing instruments, defeating the fixed rate disadvantage. The straight variable pays less interest when the related index declines. Variable rate certificates are noted by the asterisk in the table beginning this chapter.

"Variable up–fixed down" certificates are ratcheted to an index. When the yield represented by the index increases, so does the certificate. When yield represented by the index declines, the certificate reverts to a base rate that is usually lower than the newer rate.

Zero coupon certificates came into being when brokerages purchased jumbos and reconfigured them into smaller, lower-priced certificates—typically $250 for a 12-year zero and $500 to $750 for zeros of lesser maturities. You buy a zero certificate for less than its maturity price, and the difference between the purchase price and the maturity value is accreted interest. Zero certificates are excellent for tax-deferred accounts.

MANAGING CERTIFICATES OF DEPOSIT

The central issue in managing certificates of deposit is the yield curve and term structure of interest rates. Information covered in Section III is critical to selecting the maturities of certificates. But we have enough information now to understand the issues in managing certificates, and the first issue is the decision to buy them.

You want to invest in certificates whenever you can't bring yourself to invest elsewhere. If you can't venture into other income investments, hang onto certificates, content that you've chosen them knowledgeably for their advantages. Equally important, you want to own certificates when economy-wide interest rates are falling. If you're holding a certificate paying, say, eight percent, the bank or S&L owes you that eight percent even if other investments have fallen to six percent.

Do not invest in certificates when interest rates in the overall economy are rising. Most certificates pay fixed interest. They deny investors the opportunity to profit from income investments that respond to higher interest rates.

Ideally, you should redeem a certificate prior to maturity only if an alternative investment presents a greater opportunity—an opportunity that is promising on its own merits but also promising enough to overcome the forfeiture of interest required to redeem a certificate. In less ideal situations, reclaim a certificate if you need the money and your alternatives are going into debt or selling a liquid investment that is producing exceptional returns. Also, if you suspect that the issuing institution—even one backed by guarantors—is facing solvency problems, take your money and reinvest.

Another issue in managing certificates is choosing a rate of compounding if you intend to hold certificates full term. The more frequent the compounding, the greater is the interest accumulation. Investors who seek maximum accumulations must seek maximum interest rates and maximum compounding.

Investors who want certificates for spendable income need regular receipts. Larger-denomination certificates pay cash-in-hand interest, usually on the calendar quarter. Accordingly, they muster the income advantages of stocks—quarterly payments—without the capital fluctuations of stocks.

MISTAKES MADE WITH CERTIFICATES OF DEPOSIT

Both of the investment mistakes commonly made with regard to certificates of deposit are problems of attitude and orientation.

The first mistake is that too many investors simply throw their capital into certificates because they're convenient and accessible. Don't imprison yourself and your portfolio with a limited view of income investments. By doing so, you disregard the advantages of other investments that we cover in Section II, and by the time we've finished with this section, you will agree that certificates may take second place to other income investments. Many income investors would be better served by bonds than by certificates, for bonds are more liquid than certificates, rival certificates in quality and offer a greater variety of interest rates and maturities. You probably would be too.

The second mistake is to regard certificates as an extended savings account. Nearly all except the largest-denomination certificates are illiquid and not suitable for savings. Use other income investments—money market funds and T-bills—for liquidity.

SAVINGS ACCOUNTS

Savings accounts are constant dollar investments with no market risk. Many savings accounts are backed by guarantors that provide insurance against default. Since saving accounts are convenient and exceptionally small sums may be added to them, they are a perfect first income investment. They are commonly liquid, except that the fine print in many passbooks permits the institution to require written notice of withdrawal and perhaps a 30-day waiting period.

In closing, let's note that investors holding large sums in their savings accounts are doing themselves a disservice, for savings accounts pay a fiat rate that is often lower than competing rates on other instruments. If your savings account with a bank or S&L exceeds $5,000, you should consider other income investments, especially if you regard your savings account as an income generator, not as rainy day capital.

SUMMARY

Certificates of deposit are constant dollar investments with high reliability, easy access, assurance against default, and an absence of commissions and fees. Larger certificates present the opportunity to take interest payments in cash or in compounded interest. Smaller certificates generally offer only compounded interest. Other characteristics of certificates are illiquidity, penalties for premature redemption, vulnerability to inflation risk, and lessened opportunity for reinvestment.

Accordingly, investors managing certificates must address issues that we face later, including market-wise selection of certificates and assessment of income investments that overcome the disadvantages of certificates. Certificates should not be overlooked as an income investment, but they are only the first of many desirable income investments at our disposal.

4

Money Market Funds

Type
Debtor-creditor

Advantages
Capital stability
Liquidity
Market interest

Risks Avoided
Market risk
Default risk

Payment
Interest*
Compounded or cash-in-hand

Risk Accepted
Reinvestment risk

Money market funds (also called money market mutual funds or money funds) are pools of capital collected from many investors to buy financial instruments that few investors could afford individually. Money funds are the first among a type of indirect income investment that we'll explore later—the mutual fund. Such funds are offered by mutual fund families, brokerages, commercial banks, S&Ls, and credit unions. Because of their many advantages, they are among the most successful and widespread income investments.

Like savings accounts and certificates of deposit, money funds are a constant dollar investment. They eliminate market risk and charge no fees. They are secure against default risk, and they nearly always pay higher interest than is paid by other short-term deposits that are available for an equal investment. They are immediately liquid with a phone call or a check, and some of them offer federally tax-exempt returns. Money funds are available for modest capital—$1,000 is the customary minimum requirement, although some funds impose no minimum.

Money funds serve a variety of functions in the income component. They are parking lots for capital awaiting investment elsewhere and havens for investors who are uncertain about the economy and other investments. They always pay the market rate of the moment, and the investor has the option of taking cash-in-hand receipts, usually monthly, or of having receipts compounded for continuing growth. Immediately liquid, they can be employed whenever opportunity presents itself.

The main disadvantage of money funds results from the kinds of investments they make. Managers of money funds buy *money market instruments* such as commercial paper from corporations, repurchase agreements from brokerages, banker's acceptances, letters of credit, jumbo certificates, and T-bills. Some of these investments exist for only a few hours or days, and rarely do money fund investments last more than six months. Because money market instruments are short term, the returns of money funds fluctuate with market conditions.

Investors must recognize that returns from money funds are impossible to predict, for short-term rates are the most volatile in the economy. Money fund nominal yields have varied from five percent to more than 17 percent, and that means reinvestment risk. You must accept the rate that short-term investments are paying, and if that rate falls from 17 percent to five, you've lost 12 percent.

However, money funds pay the current market rate on short-term investments, and they do so without intensive market searching on your part.

CONSTANT PRICE, VARYING INTEREST, THREE KINDS OF FUNDS

Like certificates and savings bonds, money market funds are constant dollar investments—that is, they do not fluctuate in price. Most constant dollar investments pay fixed interest, and most investments that pay varying rates fluctuate in price. Money funds are a fixed price and variable return investment. Send $1,000 to any kind of money fund, whether conventional, government, or municipal, and the interest your $1,000 earns will vary, but your $1,000 will remain intact.

A general-purpose money fund invests in the corporate, bank and government obligations that offer the highest rates consistent with safety. The conventional money fund is appropriate for nearly all income investors. The government money fund invests exclusively in Treasury and federal agency securities for investors who demand the highest assurance against default. Municipal money funds invest in municipal securities for income exempt from federal income tax. Municipal money funds pay less absolute interest than the other two types, but that's because the interest is federally untaxed.

SELECTING A MONEY MARKET FUND

Money market funds are virtually identical within their types, and they have been around long enough for their managers to have become seasoned. All the money funds of each type invest in the same kinds of securities from the same sources, and this enables them to secure the advantages we've mentioned. Yields on each of the three types are hardly ever more than a fraction different from one another. Therefore, your choice of a particular money fund does not require exhaustive analysis. Uniformity is the rule in money funds.

In choosing a money fund, investigate its minimums for initial and subsequent investments, picking the fund that accommodates your ability to invest now and in the future. Be sure to check the quality of the fund's portfolio. With a fund concentrating in government securities, this is not an issue. With general-purpose funds, you will be assisted by rating agencies or by declarations in the fund prospectus ("The fund invests only in obligations rated this-and-that by so-and-so, an independent rating agency"). A money fund sponsored by a bank or an S&L is covered by the "insurance" of the guarantors that back the checking, savings, and certificates of member institutions.

Finally, check the funds' present yield and its average portfolio maturity and compare both to those of other funds. Yield and portfolio maturity are printed weekly in the *Wall Street Journal* and are available from fund representatives via a toll-free number in the prospectus.

FURTHER FEATURES OF MONEY MARKET FUNDS

Interest from money market funds is compounded continually and credited to your account monthly. You may have interest reinvested automatically for compounding or mailed to you by check every month, quarter, or semiannually. Therefore, money funds are useful if you want cash payments or the most frequent periods of compounding.

Interest from a money fund is taxable as "dividends" even if the fund invests in interest-bearing investments. However, interest from municipal funds is federally tax-exempt. For most investors, it is probably worthwhile to choose a municipal money fund, especially since, following 1986 tax reform, municipal investments in general have been among the most desirable income investments.

Money funds issue checks to shareholders, as banks do to holders of checking accounts. Typically, money funds require checks to be written in a minimum of $250 or $500 and allow only a limited number of check withdrawals without charge, so they're no substitute for conventional checking accounts. Increasingly, though, such restraints have been disappearing, the result being next-to-cash liquidity and market-level interest rates in one investment.

MONEY MARKET FUNDS WITH BROKERAGES—AN ADDED CONVENIENCE

If you hold your money market fund with a brokerage from which you buy other income investments, your broker will automatically sweep dividends from stocks, interest from bonds, and proceeds from the sale of securities into that fund. Thus, there is no dead time in your income or compounding. When you purchase income investments, your broker will withdraw the purchase price form your money fund. Also, as with any money fund, you may contribute further amounts to your fund at your convenience.

One variant of the money funds offered by brokerages is the *cash management account*, or CMA. CMA are money funds that are accompanied by other brokerage or bank like services, such as checking, credit cards and lines of credit. These accounts usually require no minimum for checks and impose no limit on the number of checks written. Unlike other money funds, they usually entail a yearly fee.

CMAs are usually offered by full-service brokerages, which charge higher commissions for transactions, and typically you must have $20,000 in cash and securities to open one. If you find the ancillary services of CMAs attractive and you are willing to pay the higher commissions charged by a full-service brokerage, you will find a cash management account worthwhile.

SUMMARY

Without exaggeration, we can say that money funds are indispensable for all income investors. The transient income investor, the man or woman who is essentially a capital growth investor but wants a money fund for liquidity in implementing financial decisions, will find money funds a movable feast. The confirmed income investor who knows the value of compounding sees money funds as a permanent vehicle of financial strategy and also participates in money funds from brokerages for convenience in transactions. The income investor who wants cash-in-hand income from a market-level, convenient, consolidated, stable investment finds that money funds of various types meet all of his or her needs.

Of all the instruments we will meet in *The Income Investor*, money funds are the most uniformly advisable. They come closest to "perfection" in providing capital stability, market-level returns, liquidity, nearly universal accessibility, and low cost. The many advantages of money funds make them worthwhile in their own right, but they are also worthwhile for their maneuverability in serving the full spectrum of investment management of income investments.

In exchange for these many advantages, investors must accept the disadvantage that money funds do not pay consistent rates of return, but this disadvantage is nearly negligible in comparison with their overwhelming advantages. In fact, it is difficult to imagine any investment program, particularly any income investing program, that could function intelligently without them.

5

Corporate, Government, and Municipal Bonds

Type	**Payment**
Debtor-creditor	Semiannual interest
Advantages	**Disadvantages**
Liquidity	Commissions*
Multiple maturities	No compounding
Range of quality	**Risks Accepted**
Special features	Market risk
Multiple yields	Inflation risk
Risks Avoided	Default risk
Depends on management of the	Reinvestment risk
portfolio	Business risk

Bonds issued by corporations, the Treasury, and municipalities are among the foremost vehicles of income investing because of their two central features. First, their semiannual payments of coupon interest generate *predictable* income that is an *obligation* of the issuer, as is repayment of the principal when the bond matures. Second, they mature at an established time.

In this chapter, we discuss the significance of predictable and obligated payments in relation to a fixed maturity. We see how fixed payments, known maturity, and market forces interact to create different types of yields from bonds through changes in bond prices. We also see how maturity and coupon payments relate to the capital stability (the relatively unchanging price) of bonds. In short, we see how the fixed features of bonds create divergent investment opportunities from market forces. Later, in Section III, we build on this knowledge of bonds and market forces to discuss professional issues in income investing, one of which is the issue of how bonds suit erratic economies.

Here, we learn more about bonds themselves—their special features, their liquidity, and their differing assurances against default—and we will note now that the drawbacks of bonds apply only to investors who don't know how to manage them.

All bonds fluctuate in price, but this drawback can be managed. Default risk is always present in corporate and municipal bonds, but rating agencies assess this risk and bond "insurers" reduce it. Inflation decreases the purchasing power of a fixed income investment unless you know how to manage such an investment for inflation. When the economy has aberrations, so do bond prices and yields, but many economic aberrations are positive for bonds. Bonds are subject to reinvestment risk. Bonds don't always require commissions for purchase and sale. Bonds pay semiannual interest by check, which is fine if you need current income but requires you to use stamps if you reinvest for compounding.

CORPORATE BONDS

Coupon paying corporate bonds—all coupon bonds—pay cash-in-hand interest that is specified by a *coupon payment*. A bond with a $50 coupon pays investors $25 twice yearly on dates established by the bond covenant—January and July, for example—regardless of its standing as a corporate, Treasury, or municipal bond.

Most corporate bonds are not true bonds, as "real" bonds are generally backed by collateral that is liquidated and paid to bondholders if the corporation defaults. Most corporations issue *debentures* backed only by the corporation's obligation to pay interest and repay principal. Bonds and debentures are binding—interest and principal must be paid.

The singular distinctions of corporate bonds are the special features that many of them offer. For example, some corporate bonds are convertible into shares of the issuer's stock. Such bonds attract income investors because the stock may pay dividends higher than the coupon payment of the bond. Thus, *conversion privileges* may secure a preferable income investment. Some corporate bonds pay a variable interest rate that is indexed to government securities, inflation, or the prime rate. Many corporate bonds are *callable*. If the issuer of such bonds recalls the bonds and retires the debt, you have to locate a new investment.

TREASURY SECURITIES

Treasury debt is backed by the U.S. government and is considered free from default and business risk. Treasuries are hardly ever called before maturity. Interest from Treasury securities is exempt from state and local income taxation, and the main differences among Treasury debt are their maturities.

Treasury bills are sold at $10,000 (with additional multiples of $5,000) to mature in three months, six months, and one year. T-bills do not pay coupon interest. They are sold at discounts from par and pay accreted interest.

Treasury notes pay semiannual coupon interest and are initially issued at or near par. These notes mature in one to ten years, and if you purchase them at the initial offering, you must buy at least five, each with a par of $1,000. In public markets most Treasury notes may be purchased singly, although for some notes the minimum is five bonds. *Treasury bonds* mature in more than ten years but are otherwise identical to Treasury notes. They, too, are not "real" bonds, but the distinction is irrelevant.

MUNICIPAL BONDS

Municipal bonds provide the features that make bonds attractive, and most of them pay interest exempt from federal income tax. Some states and cities exempt interest on their municipals from state taxation. The tutorial to this chapter includes the formula for computing tax-equivalent coupon yields for municipal bonds. Municipals are general obligation bonds (GOs), revenue bonds, or project bonds.

GOs are obligations against the faith and credit of the borrowing municipality. Interest plus principal are met from general revenues, usually taxes. Revenue bonds are issued to construct public works and are paid from the revenues of the project, if any. Some revenue bonds are backed by specific taxes, and the default risk of revenue bonds may be reduced by guarantors—a state or community, the federal government, or corporations. Most municipal bonds are rated for assurance against default, and agencies and corporations offer "insurance" for many issues of municipals.

Although individual municipals have a par of $1,000, the minimum permitted lot is usually five. When initially offered, municipals may be purchased without commission. Thereafter, commissions apply.

Municipals are subject to all the risks of any bonds, itemized at the beginning of this chapter, and also to tax rate risk. Action that alters taxes sends municipal bondholders running, so the prices of municipals are occasionally volatile because of tax rate risk and market risk.

COMPARING BOND YIELDS—NOMINAL YIELD, CURRENT YIELD, YIELD TO MATURITY

Because the prices of bonds change when bonds enter public trading, bonds provide multiple yields. The significant yield is the one that coincides with the income investor's intention to hold or sell.

Coupon yield (also called nominal yield) is the percentage relationship of the coupon rate to par value. Bonds are nearly always $1,000 par, so a bond that pays a $50 coupon carries a five percent coupon yield ($50 divided by $1,000).

Current yield is the coupon payment divided by the *purchase* price, not par. If the bond is selling at par, the current yield is also the coupon yield ($50 divided by $1,000). If public trading has beaten the bond's price below par, say to $500, the current yield becomes ten percent ($50 divided by $500) on these *discount* bonds. If market conditions elevate the bond's price above par, say to $1,200, the current yield is 4.17 percent ($50 divided by $1,200) for *premium* bonds.

But investors who buy a bond at a discount and hold it until maturity are concerned with *yield to maturity*. Such investors receive the stated coupon payment and also a capital gain when the bond matures at par. Therefore, their total payment consists of interest and the difference between the purchase price and par. The tutorial to this chapter includes the formula for computing yield to maturity.

Yield to maturity is the consequence of price fluctuations when bonds enter public trading. Bonds fluctuate in public markets because economy-wide interest rates rise and fall and because the creditworthiness of bond issuers may change. Certain wholesale economic conditions also produce price fluctuations, as we see in Section III, and these conditions, too, create the need to understand yield to maturity.

BONDS AND CAPITAL FLUCTUATION—INCREASED ECONOMY-WIDE INTEREST RATES

Interest rates rise and fall for many reasons, and the prices of bonds move inversely to interest rates. This fact is central, so we repeat it: As interest rates rise, bond prices fall; as interest rates fall, bond prices rise.

Take the case of a Treasury security that was issued to pay $50 per year (a five percent coupon rate), which was competitive in an economy that established five percent as a market rate. Five years after the bond was issued, however, general interest rates had increased to ten percent. Investors with $1,000 can invest at ten percent, receiving $100 yearly ($100 is ten percent of $1,000). The price of the Treasury bond will therefore fall to $500.

The bond was issued at five percent and pays $50 yearly. With interest rates at ten percent, investors won't pay $1,000 to receive $50—half the prevailing rate. For the Treasury bond to be competitive in a changed economy, its price will have to fall until $50 is competitive with the yield of other investments. That price is $500.

The investor who paid $1,000 for the bond is holding a security that markets have reduced $500 because of changed interest rates. He or she has been victimized by changes in interest rates.

The investor who profits from the change in interest rates is the new buyer who receives $50 a year but paid only $500 for that income. The new buyer receives a ten percent current yield ($50 divided by the purchase price of $500) and still has $1,000 coming when the bond matures.

BONDS AND CAPITAL FLUCTUATION—A DECLINE IN CREDITWORTHINESS

Digital Datadump issues a bond at par with a coupon of five percent when issuers of similar creditworthiness and the general level of interest rates dictate that five percent is competitive. Investors pay $1,000 for the bond, and they receive $50 per year.

However, IBM creates a superior computer. The revenues of Digital Datadump therefore deteriorate, and owners of its bonds sell them. Potential buyers realize that the creditworthiness of Digital Datadump has eroded, so they won't pay $1,000 for the bonds.

The marketplace reevaluates these bonds as speculative, and their price falls to $500 as a consequence of business risk. Initial investors can sell the bonds at $500, losing half their investment, or hold them and hope that Digital Datadump won't go bankrupt before its bonds mature.

Investors who believe that the IBM computer is overrated and investors who want the higher current yield offered by the depressed price of Digital Datadump's bonds will buy these bonds because the bond features haven't changed. The issuer must still pay $50 per year and is still obligated to repay $1,000. The market changed; the bond didn't.

Current yield increased because market price declined. The new purchaser receives a ten percent current yield instead of five percent ($50 divided by $500 instead of $50 divided by $1,000) and still holds claim on $1,000. If the bond matures, the new investor receives the $1,000 that would have gone to the original purchaser.

DECREASE IN ECONOMY-WIDE INTEREST/IMPROVEMENT IN CREDITWORTHINESS

The price of both the Treasury bond and the Digital Datadump bond will rise if economy-wide rates fall or if creditworthiness improves. Both bonds were paying $50 per year and selling at $500 because general interest rates had risen or creditworthiness had declined. However, economy-wide interest rates slowly fall to five percent or Digital Datadump performs a laboratory miracle.

While other investments offer five percent, these bonds offer current yields of ten percent. Investors who bought the bonds at $500 won't sell because they're earning ten percent current yield while everyone else is earning five percent. Eventually, buyers must pay $1,000 if they want either bond. At that price, the coupon yield and the current yield will again be five percent ($50 divided by $1,000). Those who bought at $1,000 have broken even, but those who bought at $500 doubled their money.

In sum, the availability of bonds at prices below par adds the dimension of capital gains to bond income. Your total return on a bond is not merely the bond's coupon but also its price appreciation. Thus, yield to maturity meshes an income return with a price return.

BONDS SELLING ABOVE PAR

Bonds may sell at premiums, market prices above $1,000 par, as you can easily tell by reading Treasury bond quotations in the financial press. Treasuries with coupons of $120 and more are selling for $1,200 to $1,500 even though the Treasury is obligated to repay only $1,000 par. Bonds "go premium" when the issuer offered coupons at then current markets and interest rates then fell, when the creditworthiness of the issuer improves, or when special features (such as convertibility) become more attractive.

Of the three reasons, the first is the most common. In the late 1970s, interest rates exceeded ten percent and new bonds had to offer that coupon rate. Interest rates then fell, drawing investors into high-coupon bonds. The prices of those bonds rose above par until the current yields were bid down to the prevailing rate. More recently, the soaring stock market caused corporate convertible bonds to sell above par, reflecting the higher prices of their underlying stocks.

MANAGING BONDS

As you no doubt realize by now, the features of bonds are fixed, and this enables you to assess bonds according to your orientation toward investment, need for income, receptiveness to price, insistence on quality, and intention to hold bonds or sell them.

In contrast, financial markets and economies constantly vary. When the irresistible force of markets meets the immovable object of fixed bond features, the bond's price is caught in between. The market cannot change your bond's maturity or coupon payment. It cannot change your bond's quality, although business and economic conditions will. The market has only price with which to express its satisfaction or dissatisfaction with your bond.

Yet each of the fixed features of bonds creates a different price response in public markets. In the larger terminology of bonds, price responses to markets are discussed as capital stability, reinvestment opportunity, liquidity preference, and quality premium. Therefore, you judge bonds for the attractiveness of their fixed features. In doing so, however, you must be aware of how the market responds to each of those features.

MATURITY: STABILITY, REINVESTMENT OPPORTUNITY, LIQUIDITY PREFERENCE

The prices of all bonds, even short-term bonds, will change with changes in overall interest rates. Bonds with short maturities present lessened vulnerability to economy-wide interest rates and therefore fluctuate less under market conditions—they provide greater capital stability. Also, since such bonds are near to maturity, when par value must be paid, you would expect them to stabilize at par value, and they do. The impending payment of par value gives earlier opportunity to reinvest cash from matured bonds. Short bonds are "more liquid" and serve investors' *liquidity preference*, which is also revealed in more stable prices.

The converse points are that long maturities present more elongated exposure to economy-wide interest changes, are further from the payment of principal, present less reinvestment opportunity, and do not serve a preference for liquidity. The maturities of long-term bonds are expressed in greater price fluctuations, for capital gains as well as capital losses.

We see now how the market responds to maturities through price. You know that short maturities are favored for reduced exposure to interest rates, reinvestment opportunity, and liquidity preference. You know that long bonds do not offer these advantages. The market assessment of maturity is more stable prices for short bonds and more erratic prices for long bonds.

QUALITY: PRICE AND MATURITY

We've already seen that changes in creditworthiness result in higher and lower prices for individual bonds. Among bonds as a whole, investors pay for quality because quality means less likelihood of default. For any given maturity, investors' *quality preference* means that the prices of quality bonds will be higher, assuming that we haven't entered a truly bizarre investment climate. Lower-rated bonds of any maturity, and arguably of any yield, do not challenge the price preeminence of quality bonds. Unfortunately, new quality bonds may have an adverse effect on the price of existing quality bonds.

Quality bonds command a higher price in the market, but they offer lower coupons because they need less inducement to draw investors. Whenever economy-wide interest rates increase, the lower coupon of quality bonds makes them less attractive in comparison to new bonds of equal quality that carry coupons suitable for the higher-interest environment. When this happens, investors can retain quality and reinvest in higher coupons by selling existing bonds, so the prices of the existing bonds fall. From a tax perspective, not an investment perspective, these actions are called *bond swapping*. Until recently, there have been tax advantages to this behavior. In Section III we discuss bond swaps.

Quality defeats lesser quality by commanding a higher price. Quality with a higher coupon defeats quality with a lower coupon, and the victory appears in falling prices.

COUPON RATE AND PRICE

Quality versus quality aside, authorities on fixed income investments believe that there is no uniform relation between a bond's coupon and its price, because too many considerations are embraced in the coupon.

One of these considerations is that lower-rated bonds must offer higher coupons to compensate for their inferior quality. When lower-rated bonds are initially issued, they are priced near par, so coupon is not relevant in their price. When they enter public trading, business risk takes over as the determinant of price. A higher coupon might be expected to support a bond's price, but if it is suspected that a bond may default on *any* interest payment, a higher coupon will have an adverse effect on its price.

A longer maturity would seem to require a higher coupon. However, top-quality Treasuries are "couponed" at the interest requirements of the moment, so we see many Treasuries of similar maturity with divergent coupons. With corporate bonds, the expected higher coupon appears more predictably with longer maturities, but here too there is a twist—many corporates of differing maturities carry similar coupons, a function of the fact that they were issued in different interest rate environments.

High-coupon bonds close to maturity will sell near par (sometimes a few dollars higher) because, regardless of coupon, investors won't pay above par for a bond that is about to mature at par. So for near bonds, maturity influences price more than coupon does.

We would expect a higher coupon at a distant maturity to gird a bond's price when economy-wide interest rates increase, yet often it doesn't. For reasons that circumvent analysis but are confirmed by evidence, the prices of low-coupon bonds are more quickly seasoned in trading. "They've got more of a floor to them" is how bond authorities describe this result.

In fact, high-coupon bonds are markedly more volatile when economy-wide interest rates change, as if investors don't trust the coupon to sustain itself. High-coupon bonds do, in this sense, influence price, but not by making prices steadier and not in a predictably cause-effect fashion.

For all of these reasons, bond authorities are inclined to dismiss coupon yield. Income investors, however, are not.

First, if you are putting bonds in tax-deferred accounts such as IRAs, higher coupons mean greater tax-deferred compounding, and if you are holding quality bonds to maturity, you aren't concerned with interim price fluctuations. Coupon is then important to you; price fluctuation isn't.

Second, if you are a retired income investor, bond coupon is one of your main considerations. In strict investment parlance, "managing" coupon rates means selecting bonds for the sole intention of securing desirable coupon payments. Retired investors typically need high current income, and this means that their first criterion in judging the desirability of bonds is coupon payments.

Third, a depression economy also demands high-coupon bonds. As an income investor investing for or during depression, you seek the highest current income from the highest coupons of quality bonds.

Fourth, income investors manage coupon rates through maturities to create an *efficient frontier* of returns and capital stability, as is shown in Section IV. By apportioning bonds at perimeters of maturity, investors trade stability and yield for an efficient frontier of capital fluctuation and coupon income.

YIELDS AND PRICE: YOUR PORTFOLIO DECISIONS

All of the considerations we've discussed apply to your choices of bonds. Yet the central issue is still to identify the relationship between your payments to the market and the market's payments to you. To receive the payments you desire, you must pay the market's price.

If you need interest payments for current expenses, your attention should center on coupon yield. Look to new issues of bonds with attractive coupons and to premium bonds with high coupons on public markets. In buying new bonds, you pay the offering price if the coupon, maturity, quality and risks are acceptable. In buying existing bonds, you pay the market price.

Income investors frequently avoid paying premiums for bonds, but that's not wise if your need is coupon yield. The bonds that are most likely to "go premium" are Treasuries with high coupons and very long terms. Income investors who are seeking maximum coupon will be better served by a default-free, business risk-free, premium Treasury than by a bond paying a lower coupon. The higher coupon warrants the premium.

If what you want is current yield, discount bonds provide high current yield, the opportunity for capital gains, and attractive prices. However, listed bonds have been seasoned by trading. If they sell at a discount, there are reasons for this. When you buy discount bonds, you inherit those reasons.

If capital stability and reinvestment opportunity are strong motivations in your selection of yields, you will choose near-term bonds and pay close to par for the advantage of reinvestment opportunity. But reinvestment opportunity means reinvestment risk. If interest rates have risen when your short bond matures, you can reinvest at higher rates and profit from reinvestment opportunity. However, interest rates may have declined by that time. The higher price of short bonds may become even higher because of reinvestment risk.

If you invest to lock in yields, longer maturities provide consistent yields for a longer period. Further, if you buy long bonds when economy-wide rates have increased, you may get a top yield at a bargain price. But stability of yield is not stability of price for long bonds, and the stable yield you get may not be the highest locked-in yield if interest rates in the economy continue to increase. If this happens, your purchase price becomes less of a bargain.

Investors seeking the highest posttax yield prefer municipal bonds, and investors who pay unusually high state and local taxes choose Treasury issues. Price will incorporate the tax advantages of municipals across maturities.

Your portfolio decisions in buying bonds are a matter of selecting the yield characteristics that serve your needs and paying the prices required to get the yields you want. The market may later revise those prices and affect the attractiveness of your yields, but if you select bonds with knowledge of their characteristics and behavior, your investment decisions will be more fully informed.

COMMISSIONS

Commissions are the price of liquidity and the price you pay for investment counsel. Brokers cannot charge you a commission when you buy corporate or municipal bonds that have first been brought to market. Therefore, you can select new issues of such bonds without paying outright commissions.

You can buy new Treasury debt without commissions from the Federal Reserve System or from any Federal Reserve bank or branch. Treasury bills are auctioned every week, Treasury notes monthly, and Treasury bonds several times a year. Personal investors submit *noncompetitive tenders* for new Treasury issues that have been "brought to auction." Such a tender signifies acceptance of the average price bid for the Treasuries by all other bidders. Contact a Federal Reserve bank or branch for noncompetitive tender forms.

When you buy any bond on a public market, you pay a commission and you pay the present owner of the bond for the interest accumulated between coupon dates. To avoid paying interim interest, buy the bond the day after its *interest declaration date*.

TUTORIAL: UNDERSTANDING GOVERNMENT BOND QUOTATIONS

$9^1/_8s$ May 04-09   92.16   92.24   +.26   10.62

The item "$9^1/_8s$" is the coupon rate. Multiplying the coupon rate, 9.125, by ten reveals that this bond pays $91.25 yearly. This is done in semiannual payments of $45.63.

"May 04-09" means that the bond matures in May 2009, when the final payment of semiannual interest and repayment of the principal are due. Because semiannual interest is paid every six months, we deduce that the bond also pays interest in November. The "04" stands for "2004," the year that this bond is callable.

The next two items, "92.16" and "92.24," are prices.

Government bonds and notes are quoted in points. Par—$1,000—equals 100 points, making each point $10. Fractions of a point are expressed in 32ds even though they look like decimals. Each 32d is 31.25 cents. So "92.16" is 92 points plus $^{16}/_{32}$ of one point and "92.24" is 92 points plus $^{24}/_{32}$ of one point. Since each point is worth $10, the 92 points mean $920. Each 32d is 31.25 cents, and there are 16 of them in the quote, which is 500 cents, or

$5. Thus, 92.16 means $920 plus $5, or $925; similarly, 92.24 means $927.50.

Dealers in these Treasuries buy at $925 and sell for $927.50. You pay the dealer's asking price, $927.50, to buy, and you accept the bid price, $925, to sell.

The next item, "+.26," shows that the closing bid price increased $26/32$ over the closing bid price on the previous day. Since $1/32$ equals 31.25 cents, we know that dealers were willing to pay $8.125 more for this bond than they paid for it yesterday (31.25 cents × 26 = 812.5 cents, or $8.125).

The final item, "9.92," is the current yield (the coupon rate divided by the current price). That's 9.92 percent—no hidden 32ds or 8ths. It is important to understand current yields on Treasury issues because they are the basis for computing term-yield graphs, the most important tool of income investing.

Corporate bond trades are reported in the financial press. Open the financial section to "New York Exchange Bonds" and look under the A's to locate

ATT $7^1/_8$s03   9.6   140   75 $73^1/_8$ 74 $+^1/_2$

This is a bond issued by American Telephone and Telegraph. The first item names the issuer.

The "$7^1/_8$" is the bond's coupon rate, and the "03" tells the bond's maturity date.

The coupon rate, the amount of yearly interest paid, is represented by numerals and fractions. To obtain the coupon rate, the fractions must be converted to decimals and the entire amount must then be multiplied by ten. The "$7^1/_8$" converts to 7.125. Multiplying this by ten gives 71.25, or $71.25. Owners receive half of the coupon rate every six months.

Payments last until the bond is sold or matures, which brings us to the "03." This bond matures in 2003.

Some bonds pay varying interest. Your broker has a list of variable rate bonds.

On the maturity date, the issuer makes the final payment of semiannual interest and repays the principal. Par value is the amount that the bond will be worth upon maturity, which is nearly always $1,000.

The "9.6" is the current yield, the coupon rate divided by the selling price.

The next item states the number of bonds that were exchanged on the given day. Bond trades aren't reported in hundreds, so 140 bonds were sold.

The next three numbers are the "high-low-close": the daily high price was 75, the daily low price was 73^1/$_8$ and the closing price was 74. These prices are implied multiples of ten. The price of 75 is $750; 73^1/$_8$ is $731.25; 74 is $740. A corporate bond's price, like its coupon, is determined by converting fractions to decimals and multiplying by ten.

COMPUTING YIELD TO MATURITY FROM A DISCOUNT BOND

Through increases in interest rates, declines in creditworthiness, and corresponding decreases in bond prices, investors can purchase bonds at discounts from par. Buying bonds below par adds new income dimensions to them: capital appreciation and yield to maturity.

Capital appreciation results from selling bonds at a price greater than the price you paid for them. That happens when you pay $500 for a bond that matures at $1,000, but it also happens anytime bond prices rise.

The total return from bonds consists of interest payments plus capital appreciation, or yield to maturity.

$$\frac{C + \dfrac{D}{YTM}}{\dfrac{PP + PV}{2}}$$

"C" is the yearly coupon payment; "D" is the bond's discount from par; "YTM" is years to maturity; "PP" is purchase price, and "PV" is the bond's par value. The "2" is necessary to obtain an average. The numerator is the average annual gain, which is interest payments plus capital appreciation. The denominator is the average annual investment, the midpoint between the purchase price and the par value. The resulting figure is the yield to maturity, the total yield received by the holder of the bond.

We'll look at yield to maturity for both of the bonds in our example. We'll assume that we buy them at $500 five years before maturity. The coupon payment remains $50 yearly.

Therefore:

$$\frac{\$50 + \dfrac{\$500}{5}}{\dfrac{\$500 + \$1,000}{2}}$$

This is condensed to:

$$\frac{\$50 + \$100}{\$750}$$

which resolves as:

$$\frac{\$150}{\$750}$$

and becomes 0.20, or 20 percent. Whoever invests in these bonds for $500 and holds them until maturity receives a yield to maturity of 20 percent.

COMPUTING YIELDS TO MATURITY FROM PREMIUM BONDS

Through decreases in interest rates, increases in creditworthiness, and corresponding increases in bond prices, investors can purchase bonds at premiums to par. As we've noted, the issuer of the bond is obligated to repay only the principal, usually $1,000, of any bond. Therefore, buying premium bonds also adds another consideration to our figuring: subtracting the premium from total return when computing yield to maturity.

In this case, total return is interest payments minus the premium above par. Our formula changes slightly:

$$\frac{C - \dfrac{P}{YTM}}{\dfrac{PP + PV}{2}}$$

"C" remains the yearly coupon payment; "P" is the bond's premium above par; dividing by "YTM" (years to maturity) reveals the average reduction of the premium each year. The denominator is the same as for discount bonds. Using the same bond features as the example of a discount bond, let's compute the yield to maturity for a bond selling at a premium of $100.

$$\frac{\dfrac{\$50 - \$100}{5}}{\dfrac{\$1,100 + \$1,000}{2}} = \frac{\$50 - \$20}{\$1,050} = .0286 \text{ or } 2.86\%$$

Whoever buys this five-year premium bond and holds it to maturity receives a yield to maturity of 2.86 percent—considerably less than a savings account or money fund—because the bond does not repay its purchase price of $1,100. Two years of interest payments, $100, are lost in five years because of the $100 premium above par.

These figures show an important lesson about buying premium bonds: buy premium bonds with distant maturities; otherwise, the premium reduces yield to maturity much more drastically.

If our example had been a 20-year bond, yield to maturity would have been 4.29 percent.

$$\frac{\$50 - \$5}{\$1,050} = \frac{\$45}{\$1,050} = .04286 \text{ or } 4.286\%$$

Same bond, same features, but yield to maturity increases because the more distant maturity reduces the effect of the premium.

COMPUTING TAXABLE-EQUIVALENT COUPON YIELDS ON MUNICIPAL BONDS

Municipal securities pay less coupon yield because the interest payments on municipals are exempt from federal income tax. Accordingly, coupon interest from municipals is evaluated by *taxable-equivalent yield*—a comparison of after-tax yield with the untaxed yield of municipals.

Look up your income and your tax bracket. Examine the coupon from the municipal bond. Plug those figures into the formula TF = BT (1 – t).

"TF" is the federally tax-free return from the municipal; "BT" is the before-tax return from another investment; "t" is your tax rate.

Let's say that the tax-free yield on the municipal is nine percent, that the before-tax yield on the other investment is 12 percent and that your tax bracket is 15 percent. Then:

$$\begin{aligned} TF &= 0.12 \ (1 - 0.15) \\ &= 0.12 \ (0.85) \\ &= 0.102, \text{ or } 10.2 \text{ percent} \end{aligned}$$

These calculations show that the equivalent yield of the taxable investment is 10.32 percent. If you invest in the fully taxed investment yielding 12 percent and pay taxes, your after-tax yield of 10.32 percent is higher than your untaxed nine percent yield from this municipal bond. The taxable bond provides more after-tax coupon income.

All other yields from municipals are calculated in the same way as yields on Treasuries and corporates.

SUMMARY

Bonds are among the most desired income investments because their fixed features and, assuming quality issues, their high immunity to default bring income predictability to a portfolio. Selected wisely, your bonds will cast off a stated semiannual interest payment and mature at a known value on a known date. Maturities may be selected to fulfill a variety of investment purposes. The fixed features of bonds makes them convenient and manageable, and special features such as convertibility and exempt tax status enhance their appeal.

Because the features of bonds are fixed, market effects on the prices of bonds create special opportunities and situations. Recognizing the central rule of bonds, that their prices vary inversely to economy-wide interest rates, you have to contend with maturity, quality, and coupon rates as they are manifested in bond prices. Thus, the basic features of bonds are expanded into such issues as capital stability, varying types of yields, liquidity preference, quality preference, and market response.

We have not exhausted our discussion of bonds by any means. Thus far, we have learned to think about the static features of bonds in a dynamic market context. In later sections, we will learn how to manage that context. But other income investments also suit our purposes, and we will examine them first.

6

Zero Coupon Investments

Type
Debtor-creditor

Advantages
Multiple maturities
Known accumulations
Fixed interest
Attractive prices
Special features

Risks Avoided
Depends on type of zero

Income
Accreted interest

Disadvantages
Phantom interest

Risks Accepted
Depends on type of zero

Several years ago, brokerages stripped the interest coupons and the principal certificate from conventional Treasury bonds and created new investments that were restructured into bonds with a par value of $1,000. They resold each of these bonds separately at a price less than par so as to pay interest as the difference between the purchase price and the par value. Investors make one investment; at maturity, they receive one payment. During the interim, there are no semi-annual interest payments.

This innovation became the *zero coupon bond*, which paid *accreted interest* rather than coupon interest. With its emergence and the various innovations that followed, income investors are now managing zeros for an equally innovative variety of portfolio intentions. You can select zeros for compounding in tax-deferred accounts and for compounding elsewhere in your portfolio. You can use zeros to exercise your preference for stability, maximum yield, maximum reinvestment opportunity and conservative or aggressive gains. You can serialize zeros to produce a known sum at a distant date. You can serialize zeros to produce current income now and indefinitely into the future. You can also take advantage of special features of zeros. Selected types of zeros offer convertibility into corporate stock or into coupon bonds. Zero coupon bonds are one of the most useful, versatile, and profitable types of investments now available to income investors.

ADVANTAGES, DISADVANTAGES, AND FEATURES OF ZEROS

All zeros are sold below their terminal value. The difference between the sales price and the par value is accreted interest.

Even though zeros produce no coupon interest, they are taxed as if they do. The tax liability on their phantom interest varies among zeros.

Zeros produce predictable, continuous, and impressive compounding. The compounding is predictable because zeros mature to par; it is continuous because accreted interest is compounded at the yield determined by the purchase price; it is impressive because you can double or quadruple your capital with near maturities and multiply your capital tenfold with longer maturities.

Any budget and investment horizon may be served by zeros. The prices of zeros range from $25 to $10,000, and their maturities range from tomorrow morning until 2020. Numerous institutions offer zeros, including banks, brokerages, and listed exchanges.

Publicly listed zeros fluctuate dramatically with changes in economy-wide interest rates. However, untraded zeros, such as zero coupon certificates, are stable. Prices and yields for issues of identical maturity vary widely, so you must compare carefully before buying. Commissions for publicly listed zeros are higher as a percentage of investment than commissions for other investments, but not all zeros require commissions.

As zeros approach maturity, they increase in price. This increase is steady for short-term zeros, which are nearer to maturity, but erratic for long-term zeros. Given the intense reactions of zeros to changes in economy-wide interest rates, long zeros may not increase in price for many years.

The steady increase in the price of zeros is called *compound accreted value to date*. Compound accreted value to date has two consequences for income investors. First, your yield to maturity is determined by the purchase price, and as that price increases toward maturity, your yield declines. Second, many municipal zeros are callable. Compound accreted value to date is the basis on which issuers assign a call price to zeros.

STRIPPED TREASURIES AND ORIGINAL ISSUE TREASURIES

A brokerage creates stripped Treasuries by purchasing Treasury bonds and placing them in escrow to be stripped and reoffered. Stripped Treasuries are "government backed" in that the Treasury backs securities from which they are derived, but the Treasury does not back the stripped zeros themselves. However, stripped Treasuries deserve all the confidence that is given to a Treasury obligation.

The Treasury does issue its own zeros, including T-bills, which we've discussed, and savings bonds, which we will discuss. The Treasury also issues STRIPS (Separate Trading of Registered Interest and Principal Securities), which brokerages resell under trade names.

Use Treasury zeros when you want ultimate assurance against default and business risk, which is especially the case when you intend to hold long-term zeros. These zeros are available in a greater range of maturities and prices than any other zeros, making them the most flexible of zero coupon investments.

The phantom interest of stripped Treasuries, such as the Merrill Lynch TIGRs and Salomon Brothers CATS, is fully taxable unless these Treasuries are owned in tax-deferred accounts. Direct Treasury zeros are federally taxable when they mature (an exception is made for savings bonds) and are exempt from state tax.

CORPORATE ZEROS

Corporate zeros, like any other corporate bonds, are backed only by the corporation and are vulnerable to default. Their prices and yields are influenced by business conditions and economy-wide interest rates.

Like coupon-paying convertibles, a few convertible zero corporates can be converted into the stock of the issuing corporation. Convertible zero corporates offer price appreciation from declines in economy-wide interest rates and from appreciation of their underlying stock, and if you convert these zeros into stock, you may receive dividend income, as is true for ordinary corporate convertibles.

Corporate zeros feature more limited maturities than Treasuries, and the phantom interest of these bonds is fully taxable unless they are owned in tax-deferred accounts. Default risk and business risk also make them less appealing than Treasuries. You will prefer corporate zeros chiefly when their prices and yields compensate for their risk or when convertibility features present access to high-dividend stocks.

MUNICIPAL ZEROS

Zero coupon municipal bonds provide federally untaxed accreted interest. The tax advantages, range of maturities, and predictable accumulations of municipal zeros have caused investors to prefer them over stocks, have advanced them as alternatives or supplements to IRAs, and have prompted investors to mix them for income or compounding.

Some states don't tax accreted interest on their zeros or on certain issues of zeros. States expect you to declare the phantom interest on a municipal zero yearly, when it matures, or when you sell it.

Convertible municipal zeros convert to coupon bonds for federally untaxed accreted interest followed by federally untaxed coupon income. An example is Intermountain Power Agency Utah GAINS. Until 1996 these municipal zeros pay accreted interest. Beginning in 1996, they convert to coupon-paying bonds with a coupon yield of 10.375 percent. About $500 invested in these zeros today grows to $1,000 in 1996 (federally untaxed), and then from 1996 until 2011 they pay $103.75 in federally untaxed coupon interest.

Nearly all municipal zeros are callable. Whether the call features are to your advantage depends on the *price to call* and the *yield to call*. If the price to call is greater than the compounded accreted value on the call date, the call features are attractive. If the yield to call is greater than the yield to maturity, the call features are attractive. If neither is the case, callability is not an advantage. You must ask your broker about call features when selecting municipal zeros.

Municipal zeros may be one of the most favored investments to have survived the 1986 tax reform, as we will see at the end of *The Income Investor*. But they are profoundly attractive apart from their tax advantages. Since they don't require federal tax, they avoid a prime disadvantage of other zeros while retaining the advantages of known maturity and generous compounding. We will see further in this chapter how you can put them to work.

ZERO CERTIFICATES

Zero certificates are direct issues of banks and S&Ls or direct and derivative issues of brokerages. Most zero certificates carry low default risk and do not fluctuate with changes in interest rates. The disadvantages of zero certificates are illiquidity (zero certificates of $100,000 are liquid) and limited maturities (although some issuers have expanded maturities). Phantom interest on zero certificates issued after 1984 is taxable yearly.

Select zero certificates when you require maximum stability of principal and when their maturities fill gaps in the maturities of your other zeros or bonds.

PRICE, YIELD, MATURITY, AND QUALITY

These four characteristics of zeros are frustratingly interrelated, so precise comparisons of different types of zeros cannot be made. For example, a stripped Treasury may yield less than a corporate zero, but the Treasury is immune to default and business risk. A zero certificate may yield less than a Treasury, but it is generally immune to market risk. Yield doesn't identify which is the "better" zero, for an inducement is offered to compensate for a lower yield. So the zero concept is simple, but the comparison of zeros is not.

Neither is the correlation of price, yield, maturity, and quality. With a single-payment instrument like a zero, price and yield are determinants of each other. But price and yield are also determined by the quality of the issuer and the term of maturity.

What we will do from this point forward is cut through comparisons and concentrate on yield and maturity. We can easily deal with quality because for any price, yield, and maturity, stripped Treasuries are highest in quality because of their underpinning by Treasury bonds. Zero certificates backed by the FDIC or the FSLIC rank second. Corporate zeros vary in quality, but rating agencies help determine their assuredness against default. Municipal zeros are also rated for quality by rating agencies. We have dealt with special features of zeros. Price is a given. A zero costs what it costs, and we know enough to make price comparisons among institutions.

Therefore, as income investors, we deal with the chief income issues—yield and maturity. When you call a bank or brokerage, you will be quoted a yield that is represented as the difference between the purchase price and the par value at maturity. With this information, we go forward.

SELECTING AMONG YIELDS

The range of yields that is available on all zeros tells us that not all investors strive for the highest yields. Why?

Convenience is one reason. A zero certificate often yields less than other zeros of similar maturity, but certificates are available without commissions from the bank where you do your daily transactions.

Fear of default and market risk may cause some investors to choose zeros that yield less. These investors willingly forgo yield for the attractiveness of a constant dollar, high-quality instrument such as a zero certificate or a zero savings bond.

The same considerations may prompt investors to keep maturities short on publicly traded zeros even if higher yields are available longer term. Remember that publicly traded zeros fluctuate dramatically with changes in interest rates and that short maturities restrain these fluctuations, at a cost of less yield than might be available long-term. Some investors willingly accept that "cost" in exchange for the benefit of capital stability.

Other investors want the highest yields, and that generally means going long in public markets. These investors intend to hold zeros to maturity and aren't concerned with price fluctuations, for they know that quality zeros will mature to par.

Some investors aren't interested in yield or quality because they play zeros for capital appreciation. They are interested in liquidity, and they avoid illiquid and stable zeros, such as certificates and savings bonds. We discuss aggressive investors in Section III.

We see, therefore, that by attending to yield, you can manage zeros with respect to other aspects of income investments—and that doesn't always mean reaching for the highest yield.

MANAGING YIELD FOR REINVESTMENT RISK AND OPPORTUNITY

Income investors often choose to manage yields according to reinvestment opportunity. Every opportunity occasions risk, of course, and we have noted two aspects of reinvestment risk.

First, we have noted that a shorter maturity presents an earlier opportunity to reinvest matured bonds but that a drop in economy-wide interest rates may preclude the same high yields when that opportunity arises. This is reinvestment risk.

Second, we have noted that although locking in yields with long bonds secures an identified return, if economy-wide interest rates increase, we might be stuck holding a lower-yielding investment. This, too, is reinvestment risk, and it applies to zeros.

When managing yields for reinvestment opportunity, income investors have two ways of dealing with reinvestment risk: select the highest yield for the shortest time, or select the highest yield for the longest time.

Let's look at three zeros. The prices and yields are hypothetical, and we assume an investment of $10,000.

Maturity	Price	Yield to Maturity	Accumulation
November 1997	$400	9.6%	$ 25,000
September 2001	125	10.2	80,000
December 2008	100	9.8	100,000

If you want the highest yield for the shortest time, you'll want the 1997 zeros yielding 9.6 percent. Shorter maturity provides an acceptable yield and an earlier reinvestment opportunity. If economy-wide interest rates have increased by 1997, you can reinvest at those higher rates. You will not be attracted to the zeros of 2001 because it takes four years of postponed reinvestment opportunity to earn an extra 0.6 percent, and the zeros of 2008 will be unacceptable to you because their yields scarcely exceed 9.6 percent and because they require 11 years of postponed reinvestment opportunity.

However, a yield-conscious investor who wants the highest yield for the longest period chooses the zeros of 2001. Interest rates may increase later, but they may also decline—as they clearly do in this scenario. Therefore, he or she takes the highest rate for the longest time and acknowledges that economy-wide interest rates may increase in the interim.

In this case, yield-conscious income investors are "right" whether they select a yield of 9.6 or 10.2 percent. However, there is a third option.

STRATEGIES WITH YIELDS—TOTAL ACCUMULATIONS AT MATURITY

The zeros of 2008 offer neither maximum reinvestment opportunity nor maximum yield. But they do offer maximum accumulations. This investment increases tenfold with no intricate maneuverings, and it's difficult to argue with maximum accumulations as an objective of income investment.

Also, these zeros reduce commissions. Bought and held, they require commissions only once. With shorter zeros, you pay commissions to reinvest each time the zeros mature. Commissions for zeros detract from *capital* because they can't be paid from coupon interest. What's more, commissions deny compounding. With zeros of 2008 available at $100, every $100 in commissions that you pay today denies you $1,000 that you might have obtained in 2008.

Minimize commissions by purchasing corporate, Treasury, or municipal zeros from the underwriting brokerage when they are initially issued or from inventory of the brokerage after they have been offered.

SERIALIZED MATURITIES FOR FUTURE INCOME

We have learned that zeros compound continuously at the interest rate determined at the time of purchase and that they therefore produce highly dependable income. You can take advantage of continuous compounding and its resultant predictability by serializing the maturities of zeros.

In the following example, we have an investor who seeks compounded returns over a period of about ten years. This very practical example might pertain to someone who is choosing taxable zeros for an IRA or municipal zeros outside the IRA for such purposes as obtaining additional retirement income, paying a child's tuition, or starting a business at a known time. This income investor wants a consolidated mass of capital in ten years, so each year he or she invests $10,000 in zeros that are one year shorter in maturity than the ones in which he or she invested in the preceding year. The prices given are suggestive, not actual.

Serializing Zeros for Future Accumulations

Year	Cost per Zero	Investment	Total Accumulation	Maturity In
1	$333	$ 9,990	$ 30,000	10 years
2	350	9,800	28,000	9
3	370	9,990	27,000	8
4	400	10,000	25,000	7
5	490	9,800	20,000	6
6	550	9,900	18,000	5
7	600	9,600	16,000	4
8	735	9,555	13,000	3
9	800	9,600	12,000	2
10	870	9,570	11,000	1
Investment totals		97,805	200,000	

If you are investing for compounded returns, you will assuredly obtain them by managing the maturities of zeros. The continuous compounding, range of maturities, and predictable accumulations of zeros make serializing them one of the most elegant, simple and profitable strategies for acquiring a predictable sum on a definite date. What's more, you can choose among different types of zeros to fill in holes in absent maturities. If you can't find a corporate or Treasury zero with, for example, a two-year maturity, you might be able to locate a zero certificate of that maturity.

Serializing zeros also overcomes the criticism that they produce no current income, for serializing can be reversed to create an income stream, as we will see in Chapter 15.

YIELDS AND MATURITIES—TAX DEFERRED ACCOUNTS

Corporate and Treasury zeros reach their fullest use in tax-deferred Individual Retirement Accounts and Self-Employed Retirement Plans (SERPs—formerly Keoghs). Predictable returns, range of maturities, handsome accumulations, ease of purchase, and attractive yields combine with the deferral of phantom interest to make zero Treasuries, corporates and certificates, and other zero investments perfect for IRAs and SERPs. Many years of buying zeros and compounding such zeros will enable you to retire quite well off.

The easiest way to manage zeros for IRAs is the *buy and hold strategy*. This strategy involves buying zeros that mature during your expected retirement and holding them. The strategy is convenient, reduces commissions, permits leisurely selection of zeros at advantaged prices and yields, and assures predictable accumulations. Also, if you are investing long term, this strategy frees you from concern over interim capital fluctuations. In fact, depressed prices for long-term zeros are welcome, for they present buying opportunities when economy-wide interest rates increase.

MUNICIPAL ZEROS AS AN ADJUNCT TO IRAs AND SERPs

Now that many investors aren't eligible for tax-deductible contributions to an IRA, municipal zeros are the investment of choice as a substitute for or supplement to an IRA.

Municipal zeros present two advantages that are not available with IRAs. First, they are federally *untaxed*, not merely *tax deferred*. Second, unlike withdrawals from an IRA before retirement, their sale before maturity does not entail tax penalties.

Municipal zeros can easily supplement or supplant IRAs. You invest in quality zeros with maturities that assure income when you retire. You can buy municipal zeros serially for maturities before retirement, or you can buy municipal zeros according to the strategies for managing yields that we've outlined. Along with or instead of zeros in tax-deferred accounts, municipal zeros can compound to extraordinary sums for a comfortable retirement.

If you're eligible for tax-reducing contributions to an IRA, you can mate tax-deferred accretion from taxable zeros in the IRA with federally untaxed accretion from municipal zeros.

SAVINGS BONDS

EE savings bonds are the original zero, the original convertible zero, the original variable rate zero, a bond exempt from state taxes, eligible for deferral of federal taxes, invulnerable to market risk, noncallable, backed by the Treasury, and available without commissions—at a price beginning with $25.

The par of EEs is $50, $75, $100, $200, $500, $1,000, $5,000, and $10,000. You buy them at half of par. The maturity of EEs is 12 years. EE bonds will never be worth less than their purchase price even if they are cashed before maturity, and they cannot be called.

These bonds pay a base yield and an escalating yield that increases the longer you hold them. Held five years, they pay 85 percent of the average yield on five-year Treasuries and never less than the base yield.

EE bonds avoid tax on phantom interest. You may declare accreted interest on an EE bond yearly, or you may postpone declaring interest until the bond matures or is cashed. Accreted interest from EE bonds is exempt from state taxes, and these bonds may be exchanged for HH bonds paying coupon interest. They were convertible into income investments long before municipal zeros caught on.

TUTORIAL: READING PRICE QUOTATIONS

If you buy zeros from brokers, you'll receive a dollar price quotation and yield: "$400 for a yield of nine percent to maturity." Zeros quoted in financial media require deciphering.

Issuer	Volume	High	Low	Close	
AlldC zr00	12	35¼	35	35	−¼

The issuer is Allied-Signal Corporation, confirmed with a broker or quotation guide. The "zr" identifies the issue as a zero, and the "00" signifies a maturity date of 2000. The trading volume of "12"—12 bonds changed hands—is followed by the high-low-close prices and a comparison with the previous close.

Convert fractions to decimals so that 35¼ becomes 35.25. Multiply by ten, giving $352.50. The high price was $352.50, the low price was $350 and the closing price was $350, $2.50 less than the closing price of the previous day.

Zero coupon municipals are quoted in dollars per hundred, which means that you multiply quotations by ten per $1,000 par. In most instances, municipal zeros aren't quoted in fractions.

Intrmtn Pwr Agy Sup Sys UT 2/1/00 at 10.429

The issuer is Intermountain Power Agency Supply System of Utah, and the maturity date is February 2000. The price is 10.429 per $100 of par, or $104.29 per $1,000 par.

SUMMARY

Zero coupon investments are among the most useful of all income investments. You can be almost endlessly innovative in using their predictable returns, attractive yields, continuous compounding, and ease of purchase in tax-deferred or ordinary accounts. With zeros, you can invest for reinvestment opportunity, locked-in distant yields, or maximum accumulations. You can serialize the maturities of zeros to produce a lump sum at a known date, and, as we will see later, you can serialize their maturities to produce a stream of income.

The versatile characteristics of zeros also include highly reasonable purchase prices (starting at $25 for savings bonds), special features such as convertibility into other income investments, favored tax treatment for municipals, and postponement of phantom interest in tax-deferred portfolios. For an investment that produces no current income prior to maturity, zeros are income investments that you should definitely include in your portfolio.

Common and Preferred Stocks

Type	**Income**
Owner-equity	Dividends
Advantages	**Disadvantages**
Quarterly income	Dividends decreased
Dividends increased	Capital fluctuation
Reinvestment option	Fully taxed income
Risks Avoided	**Risks Accepted**
Inflation risk	Market risk
	Economic risk
	Business risk
	Default risk

We have concentrated on debtor-creditor investments, but owner-equity investments also pay current income and thereby serve income investors.

Owner-equity investments represent the ownership of assets that are held directly or indirectly. *The Income Investor* will concentrate on dividend stocks as income investments and on dividends as the payments from O-E investments, although current income is paid in the form of rents and royalties by many types of owner-equity investments, such as real estate and limited partnerships. Our foremost reasons for concentrating on dividend stocks are that dividend stocks require no leverage and are broadly accessible, available for investments of any size, liquid, and are easily tracked in public markets.

As an owner-equity investment, stocks differ from debtor-creditor investments in many ways, but the significant difference with regard to income is that debtor-creditor investments owe you an interest payment by right of covenant, whereas stocks owe you nothing. Moreover, stocks have no maturity and they do not owe you a repayment of your investment capital.

Many income investors rely on dividends, but they do so with an understanding of dividend policy, of the advantages and disadvantages of stocks as income investments, of how to select and monitor their income stocks, and of when to sell their income stocks. This chapter shares their knowledge with you.

ADVANTAGES AND DISADVANTAGES OF INCOME STOCKS

There are many reasons why you should consider stocks as income investments for your portfolio.

Stock dividends are paid quarterly and thus provide more frequent income than bonds, and these dividends can be increased, whereas bond coupons cannot. Like interest payments, dividend income can be used to meet expenses or reinvested for compounding.

It's easy to identify stocks with generous dividends, for dividends are quoted in stock pages. It is easy to calculate dividend yields and to compare them with yields from competing investments. If the dividend increases, your yield increases. Even though corporations do not contract to provide dividends, they are reluctant to reduce or omit dividends. A "cultural" imperative underpins dividends.

As with any other income investment, investment in stocks for income bears disadvantages, the foremost of which is that corporations are not required to pay dividends even if they have been paying them for decades. In addition, the commissions paid to buy and sell dividend stocks are high as a percentage of dividend income. If the commissions are $100 to buy and sell a stock paying $100 yearly in dividends, your dividends for the first year are devoured by transaction costs.

Dividends are fully taxable. Tax rate risk has eliminated the exclusion of some dividend income from federal tax.

Stocks fluctuate in price, and they have no term of maturity. They will not ultimately peak at a predictable price, and income investors may reach the point at which the decrease in the price of their stock offsets the income they receive from it.

DIVIDENDS AND DIVIDEND POLICY

Corporations pay dividends for many reasons, and one reason is that dividends draw investors to a stock. This hasn't always been recognized, but research by the American Association of Individual Investors has shown that dividends and dividend policy are much more forceful attractions than most formally trained securities analysts have admitted. Understanding dividends and dividend policy is important in understanding income stocks.

Dividends must be paid from current corporate income or retained income, and corporations also need income for other business purposes. Corporations must therefore trade between disbursing dividends and retaining income for business expansion, and they do this by establishing a *payout ratio* that represents a "reasonable" relationship between dividends paid to shareholders and cash used for expansion—dividends at 30 percent of earnings, for instance.

Most corporations rarely, and certainly carefully, change the payout ratio. If earnings grow, dividends and retained earnings also grow because each of these is a percentage of earnings. This is how *regular* dividends are increased. Conversely, if earnings shrink, dividends and retained earnings also shrink.

A decreased dividend may be viewed favorably by capital growth investors, because it signifies that more cash is being used for business reinvestment. But income investors view such decreases unfavorably for obvious reasons, and so, in major ways, do investors in general. Decreasing a dividend conveys such a strong message that corporations undertake it only when they are facing the direst circumstances.

On the other side of the dividend coin, corporations are reluctant to increase the payout ratio or the dividend unless they can maintain both. So they may pay *special dividends* rather than increase the normal dividend. Many corporations declare special dividends so often that investors regard the special dividend as if it were the normal dividend.

This brings us to the singular feature of dividends: A dividend isn't "owed" unless it is declared, and corporations are not obligated to declare them. A dividend can be decreased, omitted, or killed whenever management feels that earnings can be employed more profitably elsewhere.

You can protest the omission of dividends, but you cannot force corporations to pay them. However, even though corporations have immunity from your recourse, there are investors to whom management must listen—creditors and regulators whose say in dividend policy is sometimes final. When Continental Illinois National Bank was declared nearly insolvent and its priority shareholder became Comptroller of the Currency, this regulator forced Continental to kill its dividend. Similarly, some creditors may extend credit under terms that require reduced dividends. Loans, unlike dividends, are contractual, and creditors may dictate dividend policy. Again, you have no recourse.

In more normal circumstances, corporations generally adhere to one of four dividend policies. Of the four policies, none is totally inappropriate for income investors, although the two leading types are more appropriate than the other two.

First, corporations may pay regular dividends that are raised infrequently. They establish dividends that can be maintained according to management's estimate of earnings. The dividends are hardly exciting, but they are rarely in jeopardy. Their consistency and apparent solidity serve income investors, although you would prefer to see these dividends increased more often.

Second, corporations may pay moderate regular dividends plus special dividends as warranted. This policy is observed today largely in the eccentric case of regular "special" dividends. If the moderate special dividend presents an attractive yield, you again have a desirable income stock. The special dividend is extra income.

Third, corporations may declare intermittent dividends. Intermittent dividends are appropriate for industries with long-term business cycles; their omission sends no adverse signals to the financial markets, because they were never constant, and they are a bonus for faithful shareholders. Income investors should prefer securities with consistent payments to securities with intermittent dividends.

Finally, corporations may declare dividend increases every year if at all possible. For some companies, dividend increases are part of the "corporate culture." What's more, these increases come to be investor expectations, and violating those expectations can have dire consequences for the stock price, the corporate reputation, and the management ego. At first blush, this would seem to be the dividend policy you want. However, management's tunnel vision regarding dividend increases can be as bad as its inattention to dividends. You want sustainable dividends derived from a conscientious policy and a respect for earnings, not dividends derived from a fixation with dividends.

You should be aware of two additional matters that influence dividend policy.

With increasing frequency, large institutions have been acquiring majority ownership of the stock of corporations. These institutional shareholders don't approve of dividends, because dividends are fully taxable and because dividends represent earnings that could be employed for business expansion and capital growth. Corporate management is aware of this attitude, and stagnant or unattended dividends may reflect the new facts of ownership.

For entrenched management, however, dividends represent income beyond salary and bonuses. Income investors profit from a management that regards dividends as personal revenues, but a new management will appear if the corporation stagnates from insufficient retained earnings, and with its appearance dividends will disappear.

Corporations may pay *stock dividends* instead of or in addition to cash dividends. The shares may be in the issuing corporation or a subsidiary. Stock dividends appeal to income investors, especially if the stock dividends accompany cash dividends and if the new shares pay dividends. Otherwise, you can sell the shares for cash.

THE DIVIDEND ANNOUNCEMENT

Corporations pay dividends quarterly. Each dividend is announced in advance in such fashions as this: "The Board of Directors of Digital Datadump announces a ten percent increase in the quarterly dividend from ten cents per share to 11 cents, payable on February 1 to holders of record on January 20."

Dividend announcements reveal the amount of the dividend and of the increase, the date by which you must own stock to receive the dividend, and the date on which the dividend will be paid. If you own Digital Datadump on January 20, you will be entitled to 11 cents on February 1. If you own Digital Datadump and sell it before January 20, you get no dividend. If you own Digital Datadump on January 20 and sell it on January 21, you are entitled to the dividend because you owned the stock on the *record date*.

However, corporate treasurers need time to count the owners of record. To give them the time they need, securities exchanges establish three to five business days before the record date as the *ex-dividend date*. The business week prior to the record date, stock *goes ex-dividend*—purchasers are not entitled to dividends. Although January 20 is the record date, you must own stock three to five business days prior to that date so that your name can nestle into the treasurer's computer.

IDENTIFYING POTENTIAL INCOME STOCKS

Brokers keep lists of quality dividend stocks, and financial pages identify dividend issues, as we see in the tutorial at the end of this chapter. Income stocks don't necessarily remain income stocks, and growth darlings such as Xerox have more recently been favored for dividends. Traditional income industries such as utilities and financial institutions haven't been rewarding income stocks lately, as witnessed by Washington State Public Power Supply, New Hampshire Public Utilities, Dayton Power and Light, Continental Illinois, Franklin National, and banks and S&Ls in Ohio, Maryland, and Texas. So don't believe that what was an income stock will remain so and that what wasn't an income stock can't become one.

Many stocks pay *pro forma* dividends, but what we want is *income stocks*—stocks that pay rewarding dividends. The amount of dividend is not as important as the dividend yield. A $100 stock paying $10 is no more attractive than a $1 stock paying ten cents, for both have a ten percent dividend yield. The first step in identifying an income stock is to compare its yield with that of other income securities.

An income stock should rival the current yield of debentures of the same corporation—should rival the current yield of debentures because interest on debentures is contractual and dividends are not, but should not necessarily exceed the current yield because dividends, unlike interest on debentures, are paid quarterly and can be increased. An income stock must pay more than a savings account but doesn't have to exceed the yields on certificates of deposit. Certificates yield more to compensate for illiquidity, a fault not shared by stocks. Dividends should be competitive with Treasury interest; otherwise, there is no reason to choose income stocks over Treasuries. However, dividends can be increased and are paid quarterly, whereas Treasuries have a fixed coupon that is paid semiannually.

For the present investment climate, you can initially identify an income stock if its minimum yield is six to seven percent and its maximum yield consistent with quality approaches the current yield on Treasuries.

EVALUATING AN INCOME STOCK

Having spotted an income stock, consult brokers, and stock guides such as *Standard & Poor's* or *Value Line Investment Survey*, which are available at most public libraries, brokerages and college business libraries. Annual and quarterly reports of your targeted corporation are available from brokers and libraries and from the treasurer or investor relations department of the corporation.

Income investors want reliable dividends, steady dividend increases, and a consistent management policy toward dividends. Graphs at the front of annual reports show the history of dividend payments and increases and to some extent demonstrate what the momentum is toward future dividends and whether a corporate imperative underlies dividends. A graph is helpful in making these determinations. If dividends and dividend increases track with earnings, the corporation has demonstrated a commitment to dividends.

The dividend payout ratio is provided in quarterly reports and in the section of the annual report titled "Management Discussion and Analysis." If the payout ratio has been stable or growing, management endorsement of dividend policy is confirmed.

Finally, look at the *debt coverage ratios* for debentures and preferred stock to see whether the dividend is imperiled by the servicing of senior obligations. An acceptable coverage ratio is 1.2:1 to 1.5:1—each dollar of debt service covered by more than a dollar of revenues.

If the dividend yield and these considerations satisfy your need for consistent, solid, sustainable dividends, the stock looks like a buy, and you can welcome it into your income portfolio and look forward to your first dividend checks.

MANAGING INCOME STOCKS—MONITORING AND SELLING

Identifying, evaluating, and buying dividend stocks are not the full agenda for your stock decisions, because you must also monitor income stocks and sometimes you must sell them.

Stocks often give you clear indications to sell—dividend decreases, sour earnings, deterioration in debt coverage. When these indications aren't present, less analytic factors may contribute to your selling decision.

When entrenched management is dislodged, dividends often vanish. Change in management may be a signal to sell.

Many income investors sell when capital appreciation exceeds one or two year's dividends, and this rule of thumb might also serve you. When capital gains equal considerable dividends, there's less income inducement for you to hold the stock and more inducement for you to take your gains and reinvest in other income securities, especially constant dollar securities that preserve your gains while providing income.

Income investors unload stocks whenever overall market conditions decay, the economy becomes treacherous, or income alternatives become more attractive. You would be wise to follow their example.

PREFERRED STOCKS

Preferred stocks stand between common stocks and corporate debentures and have some features of both. Frankly, there's some question whether you should consider preferreds, because they encompass all the disadvantages of common stocks without their advantages and all the disadvantages of bonds without their advantages.

Common stock dividends don't have to be paid; neither do preferred stock dividends. Common stock dividends can be raised; only rarely and among selected issues of preferreds will preferred stock dividends increase. Common stock is not callable and has no ceiling on its growth potential; preferred stock is almost always callable and has a "par value" that limits price appreciation.

Bond interest has to be paid and par value must be repaid; preferred dividends need not be paid, and the par value of preferreds does not represent an obligation of the issuer because most preferreds carry no maturity. Many corporate bonds are callable; so are most preferreds.

However, selected issues of preferred stocks have features that may commend them over common stocks. If dividends are paid, preferred stock dividends must be paid before common dividends. In some cases, preferreds are *cumulative*. The dividends of these deferreds can be postponed indefinitely, but before any dividend is declared on common, all unpaid preferred dividends must be declared.

Participating preferred pays special or extra dividends if business is profitable, and *variable preferred* dividends are tied to T-bills or determined by formula. *Convertible preferred* can be converted into other securities, usually common stock. A corporation's common may pay a higher dividend than its preferred, so conversion presents additional possibilities for dividend income.

When preferreds are callable, usually at their "par value," that value places a potential ceiling on the price of the preferreds. Income investors don't buy callable preferreds selling above par.

TUTORIAL: READING STOCK QUOTATIONS

32⁷/₈	20⁵/₈	UCarb	1.50	8	7009	30³/₈	29	30³/₈	+ ¹/₈

The initial pair of numbers reveals the trading range of the stock—a yearly high of 32⁷/₈ and a yearly low of 20⁵/₈. Most stock prices are measured in units of $1/8$, or 12.5 cents ($1/8$ = 0.125, which is 0.125 of $1, or 12.5 cents).

Next is the name of the stock—Union Carbide. Abbreviations may be confirmed with a broker.

Next is the dividend, "1.50," which reveals that Union Carbide pays a dividend of $1.50 per share per year. Multiply $1.50 by the number of shares purchased to derive the yearly dividends. Divide the yearly dividends by four to determine the quarterly dividend.

The "8" is the price-earnings ratio, which is determined by dividing the price of a stock by its recent yearly earnings. The "7009" is the sales volume in hundreds. Here, 700,900 shares changed hands.

The following two items give the daily range of the stock—its high was $30.375, and its low was $29.

Next is the closing price, the final trade of the day. Finally, "$+1/8$" means that the stock closed 12.5 cents higher than it closed on the previous day. Had this item been "$-1/8$," closing price would have been 12.5 cents less than the closing price on the previous day.

Using Quotations to Assess Dividend Yield

Let's concentrate on the dividend. Union Carbide's dividend is $1.50 per year. If Union Carbide is purchased at $30 per share, its dividend yield is five percent. As of late 1987, savings accounts pay 5.5 percent, the average yield for stocks in the Dow Jones Industrial Average is 2.5 percent, intermediate-term municipal bonds yield eight percent federally untaxed, and long-term Treasuries yield ten percent. How do you rate Union Carbide as an income investment?

SUMMARY

Common stocks can serve your income portfolio through above-average dividends from quality companies that have a consistent dividend policy and a commitment to dividends. Using dividend *yield*, not the outright dividend, as your guide, you can select rewarding equities, assess them with widely available information, monitor them with the same information, and recognize signals to sell. Unlike coupon payments, dividends may be increased, decreased or eliminated. By careful selection of equities, you have a greater chance of avoiding stocks whose dividends might be decreased or eliminated.

With the information in this chapter, you can add this category of income investment to the debtor-creditor investments in your portfolio. Income stocks bring greater payment uncertainty, but their numbers, versatility, liquidity, and dividends add flexibility to your income investment choices.

8

Mutual Funds

Type
Indirect investment in
   owner-equity securities and
   debtor-creditor securities

Advantages
Low cost
Flexibility
Many choices
Management
Liquidity

Risks Avoided
Depends on fund investment

Income
Dividends, interest and capital
   gains

Disadvantages
Commissions
Exit fees
Management fees

Risks Assumed
All risks associated with
   income investments

Except for money market funds, thus far we've discussed *direct* ownership of income securities—stocks and bonds and certificates that you purchase directly from financial intermediaries and hold in your personal accounts. One of the most intelligent and accessible approaches to income investments is *indirect* investment in stocks and bonds through mutual funds.

Mutual funds are investment companies that gather money from many investors—subscribers—to buy stocks and bonds on their behalf. As a subscriber, you own shares in a company whose intention is to produce profits from securities. A fund devoted to income investments produces income in the same manner as a directly held income investment because the investments it holds produce interest, dividends, and other income payments. There are many advantages to indirect investment through mutual funds, and as an income investor, you can have all of them, including the advantages of mutual funds that are specifically geared to income.

Mutual funds are operated by veteran market observers who are supported by staffs of analysts and add professional management to aid your investment goals. In addition, mutual funds maintain records of your transactions and provide statements of your account, reducing your paperwork.

Your subscription is placed in a total portfolio of stocks and bonds, so your investment is diversified. Simultaneously, your investment is consolidated in one place for maneuverability and specificity in a diversified portfolio. Mutual funds are offered by "families" comprising funds of differing investment objectives, including income objectives, and all of these funds are open to you if you subscribe to one of the funds in such a family. When you subscribe to a family of funds, you can move among different funds for further versatility, ease of management, and investment income.

You can arrange to have your fund pay you interest, dividends, and capital gains as spendable cash or to have it reinvest all your gains for compounding, or you can select intermediate alternatives for both cash and compounding. As we will see, multiple income sources are an advantage that direct investment can't match. For further liquidity, you can redeem your shares of a mutual fund anytime with a phone call.

In short, mutual funds provide a diversified and consolidated investment that is professionally managed and liquid. For these important reasons, as an income investor you must consider mutual funds despite their disadvantages.

The flip side of professional management is that you have no voice in selecting the securities of your mutual fund. You turn your capital over to strangers, and your investment performance depends on them. Like the securities they contain, mutual funds offer all of the risks we've covered in *The Income Investor*—and opportunity to choose the risks you want to accept. The fees of mutual funds can be burdensome, in many cases more onerous than the fees you pay if you purchased securities directly. Mutual funds may charge a "front-end load" to purchase shares, transfer fees to switch among funds, "back-end loads" to redeem shares, and "12B–1 charges" to help defray advertising and promotion costs. Some mutual funds pay returns that are classified as fully taxable dividends even though investments of these funds pay tax-exempt interest.

FUNDS SPECIFICALLY FOR INCOME INVESTORS

Your broker no doubt offers funds managed by his or her firm, but the most attractive mutual funds are offered by investment groups through an arrangement called a "family of funds." Each family offers many funds, and each of these funds contains many securities. The mutual funds that appeal to us concentrate on income from a variety of sources, particularly corporate, Treasury, and municipal bonds.

Corporate bond funds purchase the debt of corporations. Such funds usually concentrate on either investment-grade *or* speculative securities, so as an income investor your choices are polarized in corporate bond funds, although quality corporate bonds can always find a home in your portfolio.

Government bond funds purchase Treasury securities, securities of federal agencies, and bonds backed by a pledge from the government, such as bonds of the World Bank and the bonds of some transportation companies. Because of their minimal default, government bond funds have a slightly lower yield than corporate bond funds. A more damaging drawback of such funds is that, because of IRS interpretation, their returns may be classified as dividends and not as interest. Consequently, state income tax applies even though you would be exempt from such taxation if you bought the bonds directly. Some government bond funds are limited partnerships paying interest income that is exempt from state taxes.

But the most damaging drawback of government bond funds is that their loads sometimes approach eight percent. Invest $10,000, and almost $800 may go toward commissions. If you invest $10,000 in Treasuries, the commission is $100 to $200, and if you buy Treasuries at a Federal Reserve auction, you pay no commission. Anything above a two percent charge for a government bond fund is unconscionable, and you should not tolerate it.

Virtually every mutual fund family offers a fund that deals in debt of states, cities, counties, municipalities, districts, and revenue project authorities. Municipal fund interest is exempt from federal income tax. Because of their tax advantages, municipal funds pay less interest than taxable funds. The capital gains accrued by such funds are federally taxable. It's too commonly said that the tax advantages of municipal funds become greater as your tax bracket increases. However, if you're using municipal funds as an alternative or supplement to an IRA, federally untaxed interest is what you want, regardless of your tax bracket. Besides, your tax bracket may increase, and municipal funds will prove even more advantaged, as we see at the conclusion of *The Income Investor.*

Apart from funds selectively devoted to bonds as income securities, one of the most attractive types of funds for us is the *income fund.* Income funds produce the maximum income consistent with quality by investing in the high-dividend stocks, bonds, and investments found in money market funds. In short, they are diversified across categories to pursue current income from each of the types of investments we've studied.

The income fund is truly a diversified and consolidated income portfolio in one package, and it may be the most attractive one-of-a-kind investment that specifically addresses your preferences or income. Income funds achieve a mix of the securities that you can purchase directly, and in this sense they are a summation of the income investor's possibilities.

Income funds are obtainable in the same ways as any other mutual funds, and, like other mutual funds, they possess the advantages of professional management, record keeping, and the alternatives of taking income as cash or reinvesting it. We have to repeat that the income fund is an unparalleled choice, for it diversifies your income investment not only among income securities of the same type but also among income securities of different types.

Just as there are bond and income mutual funds, so too are there mutual funds whose purpose is to produce dividend income from stocks. Some stock funds invest exclusively in the stocks of traditional "income industries," such as public utilities, but most seek attractive dividends from companies across industry classifications.

Many income investors feel capable of doing their own bond analysis but feel that stock analysis requires too many investment tools, even though we've outlined the key points of selecting dividend stocks. The "dividend funds," as they are called, enable such investors—and you too—to draw income from dividends with the comfort of knowing that professional managers are doing the necessary analysis. This is sound reasoning, and in all honesty we should note that dividend funds are probably the best alternative for income investors who are drawn to dividend income. As a direct investor in dividend stocks, you will find it very difficult to achieve the required diversification, staging of dividend payments and portfolio monitoring. Dividend funds cut through these problems for income investors, and you should remember them as you consider dividend stocks for your income portfolio.

GROWTH FUNDS FOR INCOME INVESTORS

We've said repeatedly that income from investments is our objective. Mutual funds trading in growth investments does something that direct ownership of growth investments doesn't permit: taking capital gains as income.

Growth stock mutual funds invest in promising capital gains stocks and have little interest in dividend stocks. Other types of mutual funds include growth investments in an income portfolio. For example, the *equity income fund* chooses stocks that have growth potential yet do not sacrifice dividend income, and some corporate bond funds hold convertible debentures for income plus the possibility that the underlying stocks will appreciate in price.

But the straight growth fund and funds with growth components become income investments when you instruct such funds to pay capital gains as current income. As we noted early in the chapter, you can elect alternatives in payment and compounding. You can instruct your fund to reinvest all gains in more shares of the fund, just as you can elect to have some types of gains paid to you and the remaining investment income compounded. By electing to receive capital gains as cash payments, you convert capital gains into current income.

This advantage isn't available with direct investment in stocks or any other securities. With such investment, capital gains become income only when you sell your securities, and doing this obviously removes the source of capital gains and dividends from your portfolio. With mutual funds, you are paid the capital gains your shares produce, but your investment remains intact. This alternative, peculiar to indirect investment via mutual funds, converts capital gains into cash.

The ability to take capital gains as cash can be exceedingly rewarding for income investors during some markets. From January 1987 through October 1987, for instance, the Dow Jones Industrial Average increased by hundreds of points, while the average yield on DJIA stocks fell below three percent. Dividend yield was less rewarding than a savings account, but if you had been able to take capital gains as cash, your stocks would have paid handsome current income. Mutual funds give an income return from capital gains, so don't languish in the next raging bull market wishing you could take all those gains as income. You can, by investing in a growth fund and instructing the fund to pay you capital gains as cash.

QUALITY AND MATURITY OF BOND FUNDS

Quality and maturity are significant considerations for bond investors, and we must note how mutual bond funds address those considerations.

When a bond fund restricts itself to bonds with a specified rating, the entire fund carries that rating by implication. So if a bond fund specifies that it "invests only in securities rated A or better," the entire fund is essentially rated A or better, and you can approve the quality of your bond fund accordingly. For ultimate quality, of course, call upon Treasury funds, but again, be attentive to loads that exceed commissions.

Diversity enhances the quality of bond funds, for the percentage of any single bond issue in such a fund will be small. This means that the portfolio as a whole and your investment are not jeopardized by a single default.

Unfortunately, bond funds are characterized by a quirk that affects your judgment of bond maturities and therefore your management of capital fluctuation. Since we know that bonds stabilize as they approach maturity, we would expect capital fluctuation to diminish as bonds in these funds mature. This is not the case.

With an exception discussed below, bond funds are perpetuities without a fixed portfolio maturity. These funds carry *average* portfolio maturities. They announce themselves as short-, intermediate-, and long-term funds. A long-term fund may have ten percent of its portfolio maturing in two years, ten percent maturing in ten years, 60 percent maturing in 20 years and 20 percent maturing in 25–30 years. Short funds have more bonds maturing in nearer years, although their weighted average maturity may include bonds maturing tomorrow and bonds maturing in 20 years.

If you invest in a bond fund whose portfolio has an average maturity of ten years, your investment is constantly and on the average located at the ten-year point of the maturity spectrum. Your fund never matures, and its capital fluctuation is indefinite. The longer the average maturity, the greater will be the capital fluctuation, as is the case with the bonds in the portfolio.

The exception to indefinite capital fluctuation is a special type of bond fund called a *target fund*, which includes conventional or zero coupon bonds. Target funds are not subject to indefinite capital fluctuation because the total portfolio has a terminal maturity—usually 5, 10, 15 or 20 years. Fund managers simply purchase bonds maturing in those years and hold them. Income from target funds is paid cash-in-hand at monthly, quarterly, semiannual, or yearly intervals, and in some cases that income can be reinvested in a money fund or another target fund.

NET ASSET VALUE—A DIFFERENT KIND OF PRICE

The price of stock and bond mutual fund shares is called *net asset value* (NAV), and net asset value is the measure of fund performance. If securities purchased by funds increase in price, net asset value increases. If securities held by funds decrease in price, net asset value decreases.

Net asset value permits the purchase of fractional shares. If you have $1,000 to buy Union Carbide at $30 per share, you buy 33 shares and take home the remaining cash. If you send $1,000 to a fund with a net asset value of $30, you buy 33.333 shares in a portfolio that may include Union Carbide. By making the purchase of fractional shares possible, net asset value permits the investment of your entire capital.

INVESTING IN MUTUAL FUNDS

The prospectus of a mutual fund must list the fund's goals, restrictions, advisers, fees, and portfolio. You want to examine these features in light of the advantages and disadvantages we've discussed and also to determine whether the fund meets your quality and cost criteria and whether it is the type of income investment you seek. Further, if you are investing in a bond fund, you'll want the average portfolio maturity that meets your demands for capital fluctuation and yield.

If you're investing for cash-in-hand payments, you will be interested in the fund's payment schedule, and if you're letting your gains grow, you will of course want to know the compounding schedule.

Examine the fund's performance record. All funds have swings in performance, but income investors look not so much for highs and lows as for consistency, especially in a dividend or income fund. The prospectus will state what the fund's income performance has been during the past few years.

Funds constituted as partnerships and funds that offer checking privileges insist on signature verification when you complete the application accompanying the prospectus. Mark appropriate spaces for special services such as telephone withdrawal, transfer privileges, and checking. In completing the application, specify whether you want earnings to be reinvested or paid as cash. If you want both, specify which types of earnings are to be compounded and which types are to be paid as cash.

The application asks whether you want to hold certificates as evidence of ownership. There's no reason why you should. If you hold certificates, should you redeem shares, you'll have to execute the certificates and mail them back, involving delays and paperwork.

After completing the application, mail the application to the fund, together with a check or money order, and you're a subscriber and an indirect income investor.

You redeem shares by calling the fund if you've so specified in your application. Otherwise, you'll have to send the fund a written notice of intention to redeem. You need not sell all of your shares, provided that in selling some of them you meet minimum withdrawal and account balance requirements.

MANAGING MUTUAL FUNDS—SWITCH PRIVILEGES

By subscribing to a fund family, you obtain the privilege of switching with other funds in the family. As your investment goals change or as another type of investment promises higher income, you can transfer one type of investment to another by switching shares of one fund for another.

It's difficult to overstate the convenience, maneuverability, and attractiveness of switch privileges. If your income portfolio no longer meets your quality expectations, for example, you can move into a Treasury fund. If a longer-term fund no longer offers a yield that compensates for capital fluctuations, select a shorter-term fund and phone your decision to the fund. If yields on bond funds look stodgy, an income fund or a dividend stock fund may be more appealing, and such funds are yours with a call.

With material we cover in Section III, you can determine when it's advisable to realign funds through switch privileges. But you can obtain assistance in making this decision from mutual fund advisory services—fee-charging publications that review the performance of funds (including their income performance), monitor the overall economy, suggest when to shorten or lengthen fund maturities, and specify which funds are best for overall income investment. It's advisable not to be a frequent switcher, as exit fees, administrative charges, and other costs of switching add up. Otherwise, your diversified and consolidated portfolio of indirect income investments is yours to manage as you see fit.

SUMMARY

Mutual funds bring you a whole portfolio with a single investment, and the variety of mutual funds enables you to select among stock, bond, and mixed funds for cash-in-hand or reinvested interest, dividends, and capital gains. All the types of income investment that we've encountered are available through mutual funds. The income fund enables you to participate in all of them, and specific types of funds provide income from specific types of income investments.

Dividend funds may be the most advantageous way to invest for high dividend income in a consolidated and diversified portfolio of stocks. Mutual funds enable you to reinvest all of your capital gains or identified capital gains for compounding, and by claiming capital gains as income, through mutual funds you can be an income investor whose income comes from growth securities. No other type of investment offers this advantage for income investors.

Since your investments in mutual funds are immediately liquid with a phone call and maneuverable through switch privileges, these funds enable you to manage your indirect income portfolio with astuteness, speed, and versatility. So long as you are aware that fund fees may exceed commissions for directly-held investments, you can select and switch mutual funds to take advantage of the best opportunities available to income investors while employing professional managers and record keepers.

9

Tax-Deferred Investments: Annuities, Employee Investment Plans, Individual Retirement Accounts

Type	**Income**
Debtor-creditor	Interest, dividends
Owner-equity	**Disadvantages**
Advantages	Limited maneuverability*
Untaxed compounding	Limited liquidity
Range of investments	Withdrawal penalties
Reduced taxable salary*	**Risks Accepted**
Risks Avoided	Depends on investment
Depends on investment	

If you're concerned about accumulating funds for retirement as an income investor, you must investigate annuities, IRAs, and employer investment plans. As we noted in Section I, when permitted to compound, income investments produce extraordinary sums, and compounding is more vigorous when it's exempt or deferred from taxation. These retirement vehicles do exactly that—permit you to accumulate untaxed interest and dividends in preparation for retirement. Equally important, upon retirement you can convert compounded income investments into current income for cash receipts. We discuss the current income aspect of these investments in Chapter 15.

Although similar in that they all offer untaxed compounding, annuities, IRAs, and employer plans give you varying degrees of control over your investment choices, and sometimes your investment in them will reduce your taxable income. Hence the asterisks in our overview above. As we study these vehicles from the viewpoint of the income investor, bear three similarities in mind. First, contributions to these investments compound untaxed. Second, income from annuities, IRAs, and employer plans is fully taxable when you receive it upon retirement. Third, income investments are ideal for these accounts.

BASICS OF ANNUITIES

Annuities are contracts with an insurance company or related financial intermediaries. Investors contribute to the tax-deferred account, and the annuity company manages investments on the investor's behalf for optimum compounding. Annuities used to be suitable for any tax-deferred purpose, but in 1984 Congress limited them to retirement planning by imposing tax penalties on annuities cashed before age $59^{1}/_{2}$—tax rate risk reduced their versatility.

All annuities confront you with similar terminology. The owner of the annuity owns the contract and invests in it. The investment is usually called a "premium," reflecting the insurance origin of annuities. The annuitant (commonly the owner, although owners may contract for another person) receives payments from the annuity. The accumulation phase of an annuity is the days or decades in which the annuity compounds tax deferred. The payment phase is the period in which returns are distributed to annuitants. The annuity commencement date is the day that the annuity begins paying the annuitant.

Nearly all annuities invest in government and corporate bonds and interest-bearing instruments that are available in megamillion-dollar private placement markets. These long-term, interest-paying investments assure predictable returns and compounding by centering on income investments, and in this way they are related to indirect income investment.

The compounding you earn is determined by the size of your contributions, the rate of interest you are paid (or, with some annuities, the performance of stocks), and the length of the accumulation period. As of late 1987, annuity contracts compounded at about nine percent, although seven-eight percent was the consensus figure for long-term yields from annuities.

As an income investor, through annuities you can achieve exceptional tax-deferred accumulations over many years and you can consolidate compounded reinvestment with a current income investment in one package. You can make investments of varying amounts, and in some cases you can control investment selection. If you choose not to control your portfolio, professional managers will. Universal life annuities mate insurance coverage with tax-deferred compounding, and with such annuities your personal annuity goes wherever you go when you change jobs.

The chief disadvantage of annuities is the taxes and charges you pay if you cash them before retirement. Besides incurring tax penalties if cashed before retirement, some annuities impose surrender charges that exceed five percent of the *principal*. Further, annuities have administrative fees for early withdrawals, usually $10-$50. If you are disturbed by indirect investment and unknown managers, generally having no voice in the management of your annuity portfolio is a disadvantage of annuities. Looking behind and ahead, remember that you are vulnerable to tax rate risk if Congress changes laws regarding annuities.

The Personal Annuity

During their accumulation phase, ordinary annuities are defined by type of premium as *single premium* or *variable premium*. Single-premium annuities require an initial investment of at least $5,000. Sometimes subsequent investments are allowed and sometimes not. Variable premium annuities permit small investments, often $50 or less, at intermittent or regular periods, inviting tax-deferred accumulations for modest budgets. From our perspective, annuities are classified according to compounded income.

However, annuities can be classified according to the payments they produce during their payout phase. From our perspective, they can be classified as current income investments. *Fixed payment an-*

nuities pay the annuitant a fixed sum for a contracted period, assuring certainty of cash income. *Variable income annuities* try to provide higher payout income by mingling growth stocks and high-dividend stocks with predictable interest from bonds.

Retirement planning and retirement income should emphasize predictability of returns. Fixed payment annuities should be your preferred choice for current income from annuities.

Guaranteed Return Plans

Many mutual funds offer rollover annuities, called *guaranteed return plans*. These vehicles pay a guaranteed rate of interest for a fixed term, usually one year, that is higher than interest for ordinary annuities. At the end of that period, your investment plus deferred interest can be recontracted, or rolled over, extending tax-deferred accumulation. When rolling over the annuity, you might receive a lower or higher rate of guaranteed interest for the subsequent period—in short, there is reinvestment risk.

A guaranteed return plan can be useful to income investors who have accumulated funds from a lifetime of investing or from a pension or other lump-sum payment and for investors whose annuity isn't yielding as much as the guaranteed return plan. In both cases, you can select a guaranteed return plan for tax-deferred interest higher than that obtainable from other annuities and perhaps higher than that obtainable from similar income investments. Proceeds can be withdrawn after retirement, when tax penalties don't apply.

Guaranteed return plans are interim annuities. You should consider them as temporary repositories for transient, tax-deferred capital, not for long-term accumulations, because reinvestment risk pertains continually to rolling over a guaranteed return plan. Guaranteed return plans and other annuities are often available through an employer as a tax-deferred retirement accumulation vehicle, and often employers offer annuities as a current income vehicle when you retire. Such annuities are identical in their particulars to personal annuities, except that they are affiliated with an employer.

Annuities plus Insurance

Annuities of the type we've discussed are offered by insurance companies, but they do not include insurance features. New types of annuities provide tax-deferred accumulations and insurance coverage.

Universal life insurance is an insurance-investment concept that emerged after 1986 tax reform. A portion of universal life premiums provides insurance coverage, and the remainder is a "side fund" invested in bonds, stocks or money funds. Accumulations from the side fund (called "buildup") accrue federally untaxed. Some insurers let you direct investments in your side fund. Others don't.

Universal life permits long-term, tax-free accumulations that can be accessed through policy loans before you retire by continually borrowing against your buildup. Returns from the side fund pay interest on the loan, in effect creating federally untaxed income without repayment of the debt.

Even though universal life is a long-term investment with short-term accessibility, it has the attraction of long-term compounding, and that's how you should consider it. Continual policy loans diminish your long-term accumulations and insurance coverage for your heirs. The investment advantage and the insurance advantage are not preserved if you exercise the loan provisions.

Universal life is typically a variable premium product, although single-premium varieties and newer permutations have been emerging, and it has become attractive as a replacement for or supplement to ordinary annuities and IRAs. Neither ordinary annuities nor IRAs offer insurance coverage, yet UL offers the tax-deferred compounding of both. Further, UL may permit personal control for income investors (ordinary annuities don't; IRAs do) and it encourages annual investment of more than $2,000, the limit on IRAs. If you wish to take advantage of the service, UL offers untaxed, low-interest or no-interest loan income before retirement, as do neither ordinary annuities or IRAs.

Remember that insurance-investment vehicles exist at the whim of Congress. Congress will review insurance products in 1989. It has changed the tax code 19 times in 23 years. IRAs, municipal bonds, ordinary annuities, and limited partnerships have been gored by tax reform. Insurance products could be next.

Consult any insurance company or brokerage firm for information about annuities and universal life. Because an annuity is a long-term contract, check the strength of the sponsoring company. The company should be rated at least "A" in *Best's Insurance Report*, which is available at most libraries. If *Best's* is unavailable to you, write A. M. Best Company at A. M. Best Road, Oldwick, NJ 08858.

EMPLOYEE INVESTMENT PLANS

Employer-sponsored investment programs (EIPs) are often your best source of tax-deferred compounding and retirement income through a choice of investments, including income investments. If your EIP is a 401(k) plan, you have the extra advantage that your contribution to it is taken from before-tax income.

Like all contributory EIPs, the 401(k), named for the section of the Internal Revenue Code that established it, provides tax-deferred compounding for retirement. But the special feature of the 401(k) is that your investment is taken from salary before you receive it. Accordingly, the portion of your salary that you invest in a 401(k) escapes income tax. If you earn $30,000 and invest five percent of that in a 401(k), you invest $1,500 before you're paid, and your federally taxable salary is reduced by $1,500. You reduce your taxable income in addition to receiving tax-deferred compounding on your investment.

Again, we must note that Congress intends to review these products in 1989. Tax rate risk for your 401(k) may be on the horizon.

Most EIPs are funded with after-tax dollars, meaning, for example, that if you're paid $30,000 and invest $1,500, your taxable income is not reduced, as with the 401(k). After-tax EIPs are otherwise virtually the same as 401(k) plans.

Under some conditions, you can make withdrawals from contributory plans, 401(k) and otherwise. The specifications of your company EIP will indicate the circumstances under which you can make "qualified withdrawals," although making withdrawals from your EIP should be a last resort

The penalties for taking accumulations from an EIP may be more than loss of compounding. Some EIPs suspend your participation for a year following a withdrawal. Thus, withdrawals may not only cost you compounding but may also prevent you from investing in your EIP for a time.

All EIPs have one indisputable advantage: Your company makes contributions to your tax-deferred accumulations. Your investment immediately generates a return (the amount matched by your company), and earnings from your investment and that of your company immediately begin to compound untaxed. In no other investment vehicle does another party make investments in your accounts.

Corporations often encourage your stock investment by subsidizing stock purchases with average price calculations and below-market discounts. Average price calculations mean that your company credits your EIP stock purchase on the average monthly or quarterly price instead of the actual market price. Below-market discounts mean that your company further subsidizes your EIP stock purchases by offering discounts below the average market price, giving you even more shares for your contributions.

On the other hand, the customary disadvantages of EIPs are eligibility and vesting and limited investment choices. Some companies require you to work one year before you can participate in an EIP, and all companies require you to remain with the company for several years before your company's matching and returns on your company's matching become yours. No other investment requires a preparticipation period, and in a mobile society vesting makes EIPs less attractive. Typical EIPs offer a choice of your company's stock, a growth mutual fund, and Treasury bonds (for older employees, a guaranteed return plan). This is an almost insultingly slim range of alternatives, especially for income investors. More progressive companies have included money funds, option income funds, and corporate bond funds.

The Income Investor and EIPs

If your company's stock is a fine dividend stock, company matching, pricing, and discounts add to the appeal of dividend growth and compounding. You can retain the stock in your EIP for its dividends. If your company's stock is a growth stock (nothing wrong with that; it's just not our kind of stock), you'll be more interested in the bond component and contemporary income offerings of more progressive companies.

Treasury bonds offer assurance against default risk—company stock entails market risk, business risk, and default risk—and the returns on these bonds provide attractive long-term accumulations. However, your company probably won't subsidize bonds, as it will company stock.

The mutual fund option in an EIP is attractive if the fund is an equity-income fund, a high-dividend fund, or an income fund. Your EIP cannot take capital gains as cash, so the alternative available to you as a personal investor in funds isn't available through EIPs. The guaranteed return plan is usually restricted to older employees. For these employee/investors, higher contracted interest and reduced vulnerability to market and business risk are attractive.

You need not restrict yourself to one income alternative if many are available in your EIP. EIPs permit employees to apportion investments among alternatives. Apportioning EIP investments balances holdings among alternatives and diversifies tax-deferred compounding.

Managing EIPs

As an income investor, you manage your EIP by altering the composition of the investments in it or by altering future investments or by a combination of the two. In the former case, you completely change the investments in your EIP—for example, by switching from company stock to government bonds. In the latter case, you direct future investments into another medium. For example, you have been accumulating your company's stock, but from now on you will be investing in government bonds. You still hold your company's stock, but your future investments will be in bonds. And, of course, combinations of these techniques include the redisposition of contributions and holdings. As an income investor, you exercise these tools under the approach of several conditions.

First, any deterioration or improvement in earnings or dividends will make a high-dividend company stock less or more appealing as an income investment.

Second, deterioration or improvement in comparative yields on other investments will cause you to adjust accordingly for higher compounded income—into or out of stocks, bonds, mutual funds, or money funds, as appropriate.

Third, the emergence of wholesale economic risk or widespread market fluctuations warrants your flight to quality and stability—Treasury securities and a money fund, if your EIP offers it.

The point to remember about EIPs is that their chief advantages—company matching and tax-deferred compounding—are essentially long-term advantages. Your EIP need not be managed aggressively to secure its main advantages. But like any long-term investment, it must be defended, and the three guidelines for managing EIPs will serve you well in defending your tax-deferred compounding.

Should You Contribute to an EIP?

There are many reasons—tax deferral, company matching—why income investors regard EIPs highly. Add the tax breaks of 401(k)s, and it's clear that EIPs can be important to you. But, as with any investment decision, you need to consider many matters in evaluating them.

First, the tax reduction benefits of 401(k) plans are greatest for the highest paid. Second, drains on salary may prohibit full participation and the benefit of company matching, and EIPs favor employees who can invest the maximum. Third, the conventionality of EIP investment alternatives makes EIPs less versatile than other income investments. Fourth, having a sizable portion of your tax-deferred investment in your company's stock makes your portfolio vulnerable to the business risk of one company. Fifth, many people never work for one employer long enough to become vested. Job mobility reduces EIPs to a kind of employer-centered annuity from which the chief advantage of EIPs—company matching—is not received.

If any of these situations is pressing in your personal circumstances, an employee investment plan may not be your optimum retirement investment. As an income investor, you have many other alternatives for tax-advantaged compounding, including zero coupon municipal bonds, coupon municipals, and municipal bond funds. These obviously do not provide company matching, but they avoid many of the disadvantages of EIPs, and if the disadvantages are telling in your case, you can consider the income alternatives we've covered.

INDIVIDUAL RETIREMENT ACCOUNTS

Thus far in the 1980s, 24 million Americans have invested in Individual Retirement Accounts, because until 1987 all investment in IRAs was deductible from taxable income and returns from IRAs grew tax free until retirement. For three-quarters of the investors who now hold IRAs, those advantages still apply. But as a result of 1986 tax reform, many working Americans and one-quarter of present IRA investors no longer receive both of these advantages of IRAs. You may still invest in IRAs and receive tax-deferred compounding from them, but your investment may no longer be eligible for deduction from taxable income.

Like all the other investments treated in this chapter, IRAs permit tax-deferred accumulations, and for those who are eligible investment in IRAs can be deducted from taxable income. Further, IRAs offer you flexibility and self-directed IRAs offer you personal control over your use of income investments for tax-deferred compounding. When you retire, you convert your income investments for current cash income.

Another advantage of IRAs is that they are not related to your employer. IRAs stay with you when you change jobs, as do personal annuities. EIPs do not. Therefore, if you're an income investor who prizes job mobility and is eligible for tax-deductible investment, an IRA is for you.

You can open an IRA at almost any financial institution, including brokerages, banks, S&Ls, mutual funds, and investment advisory companies. You can enjoy the specific income investments that particular institutions offer, or you can participate in a range of income investments through generalist institutions such as brokerages.

Assuming that you're eligible for tax-deductible investment, the chief disadvantage of IRAs is that if you withdraw money from them prior to retirement or disability, you pay tax penalties and the withdrawal is taxable. Other tax-deferred investments, especially municipal bonds, impose no tax penalties to impede liquidity and may be used as collateral for loans. IRAs may not.

Unlike other tax-deferred investments, especially universal life, IRAs have no loan provisions, and the maximum personal investment in IRAs is $2,000. Other tax-deferred or federally untaxed investments impose no investment ceiling.

Self-Employed Retirement Plans (SERPs)

If you receive income from self-employment, a SERP enables you to receive the advantages of an IRA *plus* the deductibility of your investment from taxable income. You need not be self-employed full-time to have a SERP, and income investments that compound untaxed are ideal for SERPs as for IRAs. Again, when you retire, you can convert your compounded income for current income.

For most investors, the defined contribution SERP is the simplest, although you won't think so after reading the forms required by your broker and Uncle Sam. Officially, you may invest up to 25 percent of net self-employment income (income minus deductible expenses) in a SERP, the maximum investment being $30,000. However, your investment can total no more than 20 percent of your *remaining* taxable income from self-employment after the SERP contribution is subtracted. Most self-employed people simply invest 20 percent of their net self-employment income in their SERPs. This is an ample percentage that keeps within permitted limits and away from bizarre computations with pocket calculators.

The disadvantage of SERPs is frustrating paperwork. Each year you must complete IRS Form 5550, which becomes more impenetrable with each year's revisions, and you must complete interim forms each quarter that you invest in your SERP. To reduce paperwork, investors make their SERP investment at the end of the calendar year.

Managing Your IRA—Self-Directed Accounts and Mutual Funds

Self-directed IRAs are sponsored by discount or full-service brokers, and as with any brokerage account, you select the securities for such IRAs to be held or sold as you direct. Self-directed IRAs (SERPs, too) are the most flexible and potentially profitable. If you are willing to pay commissions, you may purchase and manage stocks, bonds, and other income investments to grow tax deferred. Self-directed accounts present clear advantages over annuities, in which you send a check to an anonymous manager for investment, and also over EIPs, which usually have a limited range of income alternatives.

Mutual funds provide diversification, professional management, record keeping, and a variety of income investments in stocks, bonds, and income funds. For many IRA investors, particularly those whose busy lives don't permit personal portfolio management, these advantages outweigh the advantages of self-directed accounts.

Indirect IRA investors are particularly pleased with mutual fund switch privileges. Switch privileges enable IRA investors, as they do all indirect investors, to realign portfolios as markets and personal preferences suggest Switch privileges are the main tool of managing indirect investment in IRAs (and SERPs). Customarily, indirect income investors move IRAs among money funds, Treasury funds, income funds, and bond funds of varying average maturities.

IRAs and the Income Investor

IRAs and SERPs put you as an income investor in a nearly ideal environment, especially if your investment is still deductible from taxable income. Every income investment we've studied is acceptable for these accounts. Income investments provide sustained com pounding that makes IRAs rich retirement accumulations, and they provide the versatility to select acceptable risks and other conditions that meet personal preferences. Untaxed, compounding is maximized.

For resistance to market risk, certificates of deposit and money funds are excellent choices, besides which money funds provide market-level returns.

Not enough can be said about the attractiveness of corporate and Treasury bonds for IRAs and SERPs. Bonds are easier to analyze than stocks. The predictable maturities and predictable semiannual income of bonds assure that tax-deferred income investors receive one of the greatest benefits of a retirement portfolio—predictability of accumulations. The range of bond maturities permits income investors to stagger maturity schedules to coincide with retirement.

Conventional corporate bonds are vulnerable to default risk, but rating agencies aid investors who are concerned about default. All bonds are vulnerable to market risk, but short-term bonds fluctuate minimally with changing market conditions, and long-term investors who intend to hold bonds in IRAs until maturity aren't concerned about interim price fluctuations.

Zero coupon bonds have become the securities of choice for IRAs because of their range of maturities, their highly predictable accumulations, their continuous compounding, and their exemption from taxation on phantom interest in tax-deferred accounts.

Income mutual funds give convenience and accessibility in a professionally diversified portfolio that includes all types of income investments. For potentially increased income, high-dividend stocks and stock mutual funds appeal to investors willing to accept some market risk, business risk, and default risk.

Income investments are ideal for IRAs on their own merits, and they are particularly competitive against growth stocks, another frequent choice of IRA investors. By definition, growth stocks fluctuate in price, and when growth stocks decrease in price, capital losses result if you sell. Capital losses are not deductible in IRAs and SERPs. Moreover, growth stocks have no predictable, terminal value. Predictable accumulations are highly desirable for retirement accounts, and growth stocks don't provide them.

General Guidance for Income Investors and IRAs

Predictable accumulations are earnestly desired in retirement planning, although the term *predictable* has many definitions. The ultimate in predictability is provided by bonds that mature when you expect to retire, especially Treasuries. At the time of purchase, you lock in a known coupon rate, a known yield, and a known terminal value. However, predictability is also available to investors who prefer short-term accumulations for reinvestment. These income investors like to approach markets gradually, holding maturities for a relatively short time, accepting the accumulations offered by shorter maturities, and looking for greater opportunities at a later date. Either approach is acceptable, and with your knowledge of income investments, you can structure your IRA for optimum levels of predictability.

Capital stability is also desirable in an IRA. You clearly don't want to lose money in a tax-deferred account. Therefore, many income investors prefer certificates of deposit, money funds, and near-term bonds because of their resistance to market fluctuations. However, preference for capital stability shouldn't be carried to extremes. If you are a long-term IRA investor, you can concentrate on yields and shrug off fluctuations in the price of your investments. If you are investing in high-dividend stocks, you can tolerate capital fluctuation if the dividend is secure.

Minimizing fees and commissions is critical to IRAs and SERPs because your yearly investment is limited and commissions reduce your effective investment. If your broker charges you $100 to buy bonds or income stocks, your effective IRA investment is $1,900. Minimize commissions by restricting transactions. A buy and hold strategy is acceptable for a tax-deferred investment, and it reduces commissions.

Similarly, consolidate your IRA accounts. If you have multiple IRAs, you are probably paying multiple fees. Place your IRA in one place, whether a self-directed account, a mutual fund, or some other institution.

Should You Contribute to an IRA?

If your IRA investment is no longer eligible for tax exemption, there is little reason to *continue* investing in IRAs. Too many alternatives, including municipal bonds, municipal funds, and zero coupon municipals, are preferable investments. These vehicles are federally tax-exempt, not merely tax-deferred, and they can be sold without tax penalty if you need the money. Many investors who are no longer able to write off IRA contributions have wisely turned to these income investments as alternatives.

Do not close your present IRA. Your account will continue to compound untaxed, and closing your IRA will occasion tax penalties if you are younger than 59 1/2.

Take a closer look at your EIP. Perhaps your EIP has become more advantaged than your IRA, especially if your EIP is a 401(k) and your investment is taken from pretax income.

If you expect to change jobs many times during a career and you are not eligible for deductible IRA investment, annuities and municipals are preferable choices for retirement planning. These vehicles are not related to your employment, and there are no limits on your participation in them.

Can You Deduct IRA Contributions?

Tax reform preserved two advantages of IRAs. So long as you're a wage earner below age 70 1/2, you can still contribute 100 percent of your earned income up to $2,000 ($2,250 for married couples with one wage earner) in an IRA. Your future contributions and your money in existing IRAs continue to grow tax deferred. Therefore, nothing in the new tax laws prevents your having an IRA, contributing annually, and earning tax-deferred interest, dividends, and capital gains.

However, your ability to deduct IRA contributions from your taxable income—one of the most desirable features of IRAs—has been altered.

Under the new laws, you can deduct all of your IRA contributions if neither you *nor* your spouse can be covered by an employer's pension, retirement, or profit-sharing plan. Second, if you or your spouse is covered, your adjusted gross income must be less than $25,000 for single taxpayers and $40,000 for couples filing jointly. Under either of these two circumstances, your IRA contribution is fully deductible.

For incomes between $25,000 and $35,000 ($40,000 to $50,000 for couples), your IRA deduction is graduated downward, eventually reaching a maximum deduction of $200.

COMPARING TAX-DEFERRED INVESTMENTS

Until 1987 and Congressional tax "reform," you and every income investor could enjoy annuities, EIPs and IRAs simultaneously. Untaxed compounding, tax-exempt contributions, and investment versatility from all three of these tax-deferred vehicles (plus the "official" noncontributory company retirement plan) enabled Americans to prepare profitably for their retirement years.

Given the too obvious incidence of tax rate risk and its possible increase in 1989, many Americans must isolate one or two of these vehicles for their retirement preparation. For the sake of all income investors in this situation, we must compare annuities, EIPs, and IRAs in three areas: size of investment, diversity and control of investment, and potential growth.

Size of Contributions

All three vehicles are available for modest investment. Variable premium annuities require as little as $50 per deposit; universal life provides exceptional flexibility in contributions; EIPs typically require only one percent of gross annual salary as the minimum participation, and IRAs are generally available in minimums of $250. The premium annuity, with its $5,000 minimum investment, has the highest threshold.

As for maximum investment, you can put as much as you'd like into an annuity. For SERPs, the maximum investment is essentially 20 percent of net self-employment income up to $30,000. For EIPs, your maximum contribution is determined by your company's guidelines and your salary, but the typical ceiling is 16 percent of salary. And for personal IRAs, the maximum investment is $2,000 per year.

Diversity and Control

Self-directed IRAs are the ultimate in diversity and control, for you manage your tax-deferred portfolio, selecting and selling nearly every publicly traded investment as you wish. IRAs through mutual funds by definition permit diversity, and control of such IRAs is available via switch privileges. Variable income annuities, comprised largely of stocks, rank next in diversity, though they are notably lacking in control. With some insurers, universal life permits investment control. EIPs generally offer the fewest investment choices, although they give you some degree of ability to move investments.

Therefore, income investors seeking maximum control and diversity prefer investment in self-directed IRAs, followed by indirect IRA investment with mutual funds, followed by investment in annuities and EIPs, which trade off in diversity and control.

Greatest Potential Accumulations

On a dollar-per-dollar basis, IRAs offer the greatest potential accumulations because of their high marks for diversity and control. But dollar-to-dollar comparisons don't really count when *maximum* accumulations are being discussed, because other factors come into play.

EIPs provide company matching. Assuming that you remain employed long enough to be vested, every dollar you invested produces an immediate return—a return that enjoys further untaxed compounding—because your company contributed to your investment.

Again on a dollar-per-dollar basis, the variable income annuity, with its component of professionally managed stocks, should be a potential high performer. However, variable income annuities are highly sensitive to market risk. Variable income annuities are therefore out of the running, for their accumulations and payments are uncertain.

With their relatively staid but predictable returns, single-premium and variable premium annuities should offer the least potential for tax-deferred accumulations. However, they place no limits on the amount of your investment. Their gross accumulations are, accordingly, in principle infinite.

SUMMARY

Tax-deferred accounts carry income investments to their peak of usefulness and earnings. By permitting interest and dividends to compound untaxed, the three vehicles we've discussed—annuities, EIPs, and IRAs—permit maximum accumulations, mobilize the manageable features of income investments, offer versatility and accessibility, and give you virtually unlimited ability to plan responsibly for retirement. Then, having achieved maximum compounding from income investments that grow untaxed, you convert these vehicles for current income when you retire.

Whether investing directly or indirectly, you and every other income investor can follow multiple strategies to obtain the full advantages of income investments. And one of the chief advantages is that income investments in tax-deferred accounts can allow you as an income investor to make retirement the most lucrative part of your life.

10

Options, International Securities, and Precious Metals

Thus far in Section II, we've covered all of the conventional income investments that you can muster in achieving your portfolio objectives. With understanding of the features of these income investments and knowledge of their movements in financial markets, you can employ every income investment we've discussed for compounding or cash income.

With these customary income investments in our bag of understanding, in this final chapter of Section II we can look at special alternatives that financial markets have created to add income to your investments. Beyond interest or dividends cast off by stocks or bonds, income securities have become *sources* of additional income as a result of innovations in financial markets. We will look at three such innovations that you can employ in your portfolio: publicly listed call options, international investments, and precious metals.

PUBLICLY LISTED CALL OPTIONS

Income investors who own stocks from AT&T to Zayre can receive additional income by *writing* publicly listed call options. Beyond the dividends that income stocks provide, call options are a supplemental payment if you will permit other investors the option to buy your stocks.

Call options apply to hundreds of stocks and are traded through brokers and exchanges like stocks and bonds. Every call has two parties: someone who buys the call and someone who writes the call. As an income investor, you want to write calls on your stocks.

A call gives its *purchaser* the right to buy 100 shares of a stock at a specific price during a specific period, regardless of the market price. The income investor who writes a call undertakes the obligation to sell stock at a specific price during a specific period, regardless of the market price. For undertaking this obligation, you receive a cash payment—a *premium*—from the purchaser.

Features of Calls

The price at which purchasers of calls may *exercise* their right to buy stock is the *strike price*, which is also the price at which you as a writer of calls must sell the stock.

The *expiration date* is the date after which the purchaser's right expires and your obligation expires.

Here's a fictitious but representative quotation for calls of Digital Datadump as they might be printed in the financial pages:

Option and NYSE Close	Strike Price	Calls–Last		
		July	Oct	Jan
DDP	15	r	5	r
17¹/₄	20	¹/₂	1	1¹/₂
17¹/₄	25	s	¹/₄	⁵/₁₆

The first column names the stock to which the call applies— Digital Datadump—and the closing price of the stock, $17.25 per share.

The second column identifies the strike price, the price of the stock at which the call may be exercised. Purchasers of the call can buy 100 shares of Digital Datadump at $15, $20, or $25 per share, depending on which call they bought. Writers of the call must sell 100 shares at $15, $20, or $25 per share, depending on which call they wrote.

Next are the premiums for calls. Each premium pertains to a call expiring in a specific month, 90 days distant from the closest—July, October, and January. At 4 P.M. New York time on the third Friday of those months, Digital Datadump calls expire. From the instant of purchase to the hour of expiration, buyers may exercise their call and writers must deliver their shares at the strike price.

Determinants of Premium

The longer the buyer has the right to exercise a call, the higher is the premium. From the writer's view, the longer your obligation to sell, the higher is the premium. The above example confirms these time relationships.

Convert fractions to decimals, multiply by 100, and add a dollar sign. Purchasers of "July 20 calls" pay $50 for the right to purchase 100 shares of Digital Datadump for $20 per share until the third week in July. You receive $50 for the obligation to sell at that price for that period. These conditions also pertain to "October 20 calls" and "January 20 calls," except that the premium increases with time.

(The "r" means that the call wasn't traded that day; the "s" indicates that a call has been canceled by the exchange.)

The closer the strike price to the market price of the stock, the higher will be the premium. The market price of Digital Datadump is $17.25. Looking still at calls expiring in October, the premium to purchase at $15 is $500, the premium to purchase at $20 is $100, and the premium to purchase at $25 is $25.

With the market price at $17.25, a call with a strike price of $15 is "in the money," one with a strike price of $20 is approximately "on the money," and one with a strike price of $25 is "out of the money."

Purchasers of calls profit when the market price of the stock increases above the strike price. Purchasers can claim the stock at the strike price (now below the market price) and sell it for a price higher than the price they paid. They may also hold the stock or sell the call and take gains from the call itself.

Writers profit from calls in many ways. They receive the premium regardless of what happens to the price of the stock, and can make strategic use of calls to obtain other advantages.

A Review of Calls

The Buyer	The Writer
Purchases the right to buy 100 shares of a stock at a set price for a fixed period, regardless of the market price	Must sell 100 shares of a stock at a set price for a fixed period, regardless of the market price
Pays the call premium plus commissions	Receives the call premium minus commissions as cash
Hopes the representative stock will increase in price or that the call will increase in price	Wants the premium as an "extra dividend"
Exercises the call by paying the strike price minus commissions for the representative stock	Sells his or her stock by receiving the strike price minus commissions
Receives no dividends from the representative stock while the call is in force	Receives all dividends from the representative stock while the call is in force

---

The longer the call is in force, the higher is the premium paid by the purchaser and received by the writer.

The nearer the strike price to the market price of the stock, the higher is the premium paid by the purchaser and received by the writer.

Whether the call is exercised or expires, the writer keeps the premium. In both cases, the purchaser relinquishes the premium.

The Income Investor—Writing Calls

Just as the buyer phoned a broker and bought the call, the writer phoned a broker and said, "I'd like to write an October 15 call on 100 shares of Digital Datadump. In exchange for a premium, I will sell someone 100 shares of Digital Datadump at $15 per share between now and the third week of October" (also July or January).

The broker executes the transaction and mails the writer a check for the premium. Such cash-in-hand premiums generate additional current income from holdings of common stock. In addition, income investors receive the dividends that the stock pays while the call is unexercised.

Apart from writing a call for "extra dividends" on a dividend-paying stock, you might write a call for "dividends" on a stock that doesn't pay them.

We noted that a decreased dividend is sometimes viewed positively by growth investors. Writing calls enables income investors, whose dead dividend is discouraging, to profit from the expectations of growth investors.

An example is International Minerals & Chemical Corp. Formerly an attractive dividend stock, IMC was forced to reduce its dividend. Normally, this action drives income investors to sell. However, IMC is an option stock, and growth investors believed that reduced dividends portended greater capital investment and therefore potential capital gains. These investors began to buy IMC stock, and its price therefore increased. The income investor who wrote a call on IMC received handsome premiums to offset the reduced dividend.

In many cases, purchasers of IMC calls exercised, and writers had to sell. This pleased income investors, for IMC was no longer a dividend investment. They pocketed the premium and reinvested the proceeds of the stock sale in income securities. Calls created income for them and disengaged them from a stock they no longer wanted.

Further Uses for Calls

Writing calls generates income from stocks that are falling in price. Let's say that the price of your dividend stock is falling but that you believe the dividend is secure. You can keep the dividends the stock pays and write a call for extra income, thus compensating for the falling price. If the market price falls below the strike price, the call will probably not be exercised.

Income investors must decide to write in the money, on the money, or out of the money. In-the-money and on-the-money calls provide greater premium income. Out-of-the-money calls generate less premium but reduce the chances of the stock's being called. Income investors must also decide how long to be vulnerable to a call. Longer calls require longer vulnerability but generate greater premium income.

In making price and expiration decisions, assess the stock's potential as a dividend investment. If the dividends appear secure, you might not want to risk the call's being exercised. Write out of the money with brief expiration—less premium, but you don't want to lose the stock.

Look at alternative income investments. Perhaps your present dividend yield is not as attractive as other yields. Disposing of the stock enables you to reinvest elsewhere. Select on-the-money calls for greater premium and for a greater chance of the stock being called.

Write in the money if the stock price is likely to decline and the dividend is secure. The higher premium from an in-the-money call rewards your judgment if the stock falls below the exercise price, because you keep the higher premium, the stock, and its dividends. The choice of a longer or shorter expiration date is up to you.

You can buy a call back if you haven't received an exercise notice. Phone the broker with whom you wrote the call and say, "I've written a call, and I want to buy it back."

Your every move with calls requires commissions—lots of them. Commissions can be a deterrent to writing calls, but the additional income from your stocks and the opportunity to use calls in strategies for retaining and disposing of stocks may make your commissions worth their cost.

INCOME FROM FOREIGN INVESTMENTS

The main advantage of foreign investments is *currency translation*— the possibility that the currency of a foreign investment will appreciate against the dollar, producing greater returns when the currency is translated back into dollars.

For example, investors who placed capital into a Swiss savings account in the early 1970s, when $3 bought nine Swiss francs, were greatly pleased five years later, when nine Swiss francs equaled $6.

Currency translation isn't always advantageous. A few years ago, $1 purchased 60 Spanish pesetas. Today 60 Spanish pesetas are worth about $0.30.

The most straightforward strategy for income investors seeking foreign interest is to open a savings account or purchase a certificate of deposit with an offshore bank—and "offshore" includes Canada and Mexico, as well as the Grand Cayman Islands and England. Income investors may hold deposits abroad in U.S. dollars or another currency, such as a savings account in Switzerland held in French francs, British pounds, German marks, or Canadian dollars. Interest is usually paid in the currency held. If that currency appreciates against the dollar, interest and principal benefit from currency translation when it is converted back to dollars.

Foreign depository institutions operate like their American counterparts, except that their account fees may be greater, their minimum investments may be higher (often at least $5,000), and their interest may be less, particularly if you invest less than $100,000. Accordingly, currency translation becomes your chief source of income.

Remember that investing offshore accepts political risk when you expatriate capital. Investors who held deposits in Mexico, for example, received 20 percent interest until Mexico devalued its peso and wiped out all of the interest gained and much of the principal invested.

Income from Foreign Stocks and Bonds

In 1970 the U.S. market share of world securities, stocks and bonds, was 66 percent. By 1987 the figure was 45 percent. Income investors have found foreign markets to be lucrative sources of interest and dividends.

American investors can purchase stock in foreign companies traded on U.S. exchanges—for example, SONY Corporation on the New York Stock Exchange. American-listed foreign stocks are issued as American Depository Receipts, or ADRs, which represent an equity investment in a foreign firm through U.S. exchanges. ADRs are liquid, just like stocks, pay dividends in U.S. dollars, and are purchased and sold in U.S. dollars. ADRs are not true international investments, but they represent an international profit potential, including the potential for American income investors to profit from the dividend increases of foreign firms.

Income investors can purchase stocks directly from foreign exchanges through a U.S. broker who uses his or her firm's international desk for transactions on say, the Paris Bourse. In this case, all the transactions are in the currency of the host country, as are all the payments, which must be translated back to dollars, potentially for a currency gain from dividends.

The same holds true for foreign bonds. You can purchase them when they're occasionally marketed in the United States, or you can instruct your broker to buy them in Finland or Sweden or wherever. Your interest return and principal repayment will be in the currency of the issuer. This may or may not be the case if you buy foreign bonds retailed in the United States, for when foreign firms and nations enter U.S. capital markets, they can opt to pay returns in their currency or ours.

Performance of international mutual funds and unit trusts has been exceptional. In 1986, for instance, international funds averaged a 43 percent total return (interest, dividends, and capital gains), compared to the 16 percent average of all mutual funds. Currency swings have been responsible for much of this performance, and they are reflected in the net asset value of your fund, which conveniently translates payments into dollars for you.

Income from Foreign Annuities

Foreign insurance companies, particularly in Switzerland, offer annuities similar in nearly all respects to American products, including single-premium or variable premium and fixed payment or variable payment varieties.

Your premiums are paid in the host insurer's currency. During the annuity's accumulation phase, that currency may appreciate against the dollar and, of course, your premiums compound tax-deferred from investments by the insurer. During the payout phase, you may receive greater returns when the host currency is reconverted to dollars.

The disadvantage is that the premiums must be paid in the currency of the insurer. You must, for example, convert dollars to Swiss francs when making your annuity investment in Switzerland. If you choose a variable premium annuity that involves investments over many years, you have to invest more dollars if the host currency appreciates while you're investing. In that case, currency translation works against you.

PRECIOUS METALS AS AN INCOME INVESTMENT

From the standpoint of income investors, a crucial drawback of gold and silver is that they produce no current income for cash or compounding. Many investors, even income investors, own precious metals, but confirmed income investors are interested in earning income from metals.

If you hold precious metals, ask your broker about *customer-granted options*. These new instruments, like the stock options we discussed earlier, feature strike prices and expiration periods and can be used by metals-holding income investors to write call options for income.

As with any call, the purchaser of the call pays the holder of the metals a premium for writing the call. The writer may spend the premium as he or she wishes. Of course, if the market price of the metals exceeds the strike price of the call, the owner of the metals must sell.

The simplest way to have both precious metals and income is to buy mutual funds that concentrate on metals stocks. These funds offer all of the advantages we've noted, and they are indirect investments that provide a position in precious metals without the burdens and costs and taxes of receiving bullion personally, insuring it, and storing it. The fortunes of metals funds reflect the fortunes of metals, much as when you hold metals personally, but the funds pay dividends (a few pay gold coins as dividends).

Another alternative is bonds that are metals surrogates. Such issues as the bonds of Sunshine Mining Company are conventional interest-bearing bonds, yet the investor has the alternative of taking the principal in silver or par value. The bond covenant specifies the number of ounces represented by the par value. With some metals surrogates, bond investors may convert their bonds into metals before the bonds mature.

SUMMARY

As an income investor, you can take advantage of additional income possibilities from stock ownership, investment abroad, and a variety of investments that mate income with ownership of precious metals. These income kicker investments represent numerous alternatives for cash payments now and in the future, afford you higher potential returns from currency swings, and expand income possibilities into areas that normally are not known for current income, such as precious metals. As you expand your acquaintance with income investments and your sophistication in managing them, these alternatives—and other income alternatives that will become available in the financial future—can produce the income and the satisfaction that their potential suggests.

SECTION

III

The Professional
Income Investor

We could call *The Income Investor* to a halt here, and you have enough information to be a successful income investor. We've looked at the nature of investment and income investment. We've identified the risks and rewards of income investing. We've reviewed how individual income investments can be managed to avoid many risks and to profit from the risks we do accept. We know about yield and compounding and capital stability and the quality and maturity of income investments. Section III carries that knowledge and us into the realm of genuine competence in employing income investments during investment and life situations.

The following chapter examines the foremost tool of income investing—the yield curve and term structure of interest rates. The term-yield graph enables us to compare the characteristics and yields of income investments against the economy-wide rate of interest, and it also enables us to mobilize income investments for erratic economies.

We have discussed economic risk in passing, but in Section III we address economic risk and income investments at length, with chapters devoted to managing income investments during inflation, recession, and depression.

We have also made slight mention of transient and aggressive income investors. In Section III we consider them more fully and show what all income investors can learn from them.

Income investments bulk large in the portfolios of retired investors. In Chapter 15 we complete our coverage of tax-deferred income investments by suggesting how they should be converted to current income for retirement.

Section III puts everything from Sections I and II together. Now we aren't merely studying income investments or examining their advantages and disadvantages or even learning how to manage them singly. Now we're going to learn how to *manage portfolios* of income investments. This section of *The Income Investor* takes you beyond a basic understanding into full competence in managing your income investments. This is what the pros know.

11

The Yield Curve and Term Structure of Interest Rates

We've often noted that an economy presents economy-wide rates of interest and that we must evaluate the risks, features, and yields of individual income investments against those economy-wide rates. We now clarify what we mean by "economy-wide."

Many rates of interest could claim to be "the" economy-wide rate—the prime rate charged by banks, the discount rate charged by the Federal Reserve, the home mortgage or credit card interest rate. But these rates are not "the" economy-wide rate to income investors for several reasons: they are established by dictate; they are only indirectly related to personal investment markets; they apply to differing sectors of the economy; and, more suggestively, they define interest as payments rather than as income received.

According to the consensus of income investors and of macroeconomists, the economy-wide rate of interest refers to the *yield curve* and *term structure of interest rates* represented by the current yields of Treasury securities at stated maturities. The economy-wide interest rate is so defined because Treasuries yields are free from the effects of default and business risk, are not centered on a single eco-

nomic sector, are not consumption based, directly capture investment payments, and reflect market forces that have adjusted stated
coupon yields through price changes.

Accordingly, employing Treasury yields as a standard refines
our recognition of economy-wide interest rates in a way that is particularly useful to income investors.

CONSTRUCTING THE TERM-YIELD GRAPH

On paper, draw a vertical axis and an intersecting horizontal axis.
Label the vertical axis "Y" for current yield and the horizontal axis
"T" for time.

Refer to the final entry behind each bond in the "Treasuries" section of the newspaper. That entry is the current yield, as we saw in
our tutorial on bonds (see Chapter 5). Do not use the coupon rate.

Divide the horizontal axis into two-year or three-year intervals.
For each period, select a Treasury security and "X" its current yield
against the vertical axis. It doesn't matter which Treasury security
you choose, for market forces cause the current yield to be nearly
identical at each maturity even if coupons differ.

Draw a line connecting the X's.

The X's are the term structure of interest rates. They indicate the
rate of interest that is paid for "risk free" investments at varying
terms of maturity.

The line connecting the X's is the yield curve. The yield curve
links the discrete points in the term structure into a progression and
shows the breakpoint in the term structure—the yield elbow.

In our example (Figure 11-1), yields increase over 14 years, after
which they plateau, then decline. That point of decline is the yield
elbow. Regardless of where it appears, the yield elbow indicates the
maturity at which the economy offers the highest yield—14 years in
this case. The yield curve also indicates the maturity beyond which
the economy does not offer higher yields to reward investing longer
term.

The term structure and yield curve don't explain *why* yields
won't increase indefinitely, why the yield elbow appears where it
does, why the years beyond the yield elbow offer a declining yield,

---

FIGURE 11–1   Yield Curve and Term Structure of Interest Rates

---

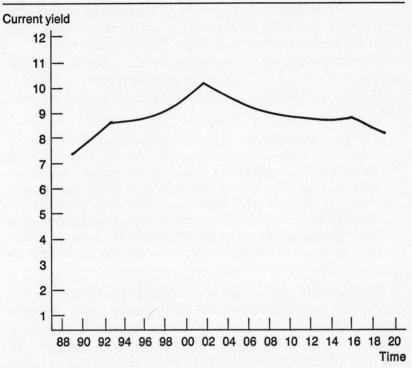

and why there is sometimes no yield elbow. Conditions in the general economy may be the answer. Social psychology or consumer psychology or investor expectations may be the answer. Maybe securities markets are expressing their own aberrations and ignoring any of these possibilities. The term structure and yield curve give you a picture, not an explanation, but it is a useful picture.

The term-yield graph is the basis for comparing all income investments *because the graph holds three factors constant.*

Quality is constant as the highest obtainable because the graph is based on Treasury securities. Every investment other than Treasury securities is lower in quality.

Term of maturity is constant because the graph identifies each maturity specifically. Thus, a Treasury of that maturity may be compared with any investment of like maturity.

Yield is constant with respect to quality and maturity (at least on the day you drew the graph) because the graph fixes a day in time and identifies the highest-quality yield that is available on that day. Every comparison yield of a similar maturity must justify itself against the highest-quality yield of the Treasury maturity.

The term-yield graph is an *absolute meridian* of quality, term of maturity, and yield; it is *the* standard in quality, term, and yield—no argument, no contradiction, no exceptions. We look at the term-yield graph, and we can say:

> This graph shows me the highest-quality investment that this economy offers. It shows me the maturities that are available in the highest-quality investment. It shows me the current yield of the highest-quality investment at each maturity. It shows me *the* investment that addresses these three factors. No other investment can match all three of the factors I see on this graph. I can and must compare every investment against these standards. *If a particular investment cannot give me what I see here, that investment must offer me another inducement to buy it.*

The term-yield graph enables us to isolate the effects of every consideration we've studied—market risk, business risk, economic risk, reinvestment risk, inflation risk, tax rate risk, liquidity, yield, maturity, quality—everything. Being able to isolate the effects of these risks, we can determine whether we accept the risks and what compensation we require for accepting them.

To express the situation as an economist would, the term-yield graph enables us to isolate variables for study by holding other considerations constant at the highest standards. By using the term-yield graph, we can:

- Estimate reinvestment risk by establishing the time frame in which an economy is yielding its highest rates.
- Select intelligent maturities and diversify them.
- Evaluate market risk, interest rate risk, liquidity, and opportunity for a single investment.
- Decide among multiple income investments on the basis of quality, yield, risk, and opportunity.
- Assist in the deciding whether to sell an investment based on a comparison with competing investments.

- Assist in the deciding whether to consume income rather than invest.
- Assess the economy and deal with economic risk, as we will in the following chapters.

That is a powerful set of claims for one simple graph requiring five minutes to draw, but the term-yield graph delivers. Refer to Figure 11–1 again. Now let's use it for assessing income investments.

IDENTICAL MATURITIES—ASSESSING QUALITY AND YIELD

No investment is as immune to default risk and market risk as Treasuries. Any other investment must offer something to compensate for the quality differential.

To illustrate: A bond from IBM offers $8^1/_2$ percent current yield for maturity in 1992. Referring to Figure 11–1, Treasuries of 1992 offer the same current yield. IBM is a solid company, but it presents default risk, however minimal. Do you buy the Treasury bond or the IBM?

Unless the IBM bond provides you another inducement, convertibility perhaps, you have no reason to prefer it over the default-free Treasury. And if a bond from another corporation can't even match the Treasury yield, it had better have a whopping inducement to commend it. The term-yield graph helped us make this choice in managing quality and yield.

ASSESSING LIQUIDITY, MARKET RISK, AND REINVESTMENT RISK

Let's use Figure 11–1 to judge two issues of identical quality, both Treasuries. The problem will be assessing liquidity and market risk.

The Treasury issues of 1994 and 2008 offer about the same current yield—a bit under nine percent. As regards yield and quality, these bonds are identical. The term-yield graph judges between any two income investments presenting this situation.

First, when yields are undifferentiated, you typically prefer a shorter maturity to a longer. The shorter maturity of the former gives you the opportunity to reinvest sooner, thus perhaps taking advantage of potentially higher economy-wide interest in 1994. Like most investors, you have a liquidity preference for the shorter bond because it presents you with reinvestment opportunity sooner. (Both bonds are equally salable and equally liquid, but the shorter bond is doubly liquid because it matures sooner.)

Second, although Treasuries are immune to default risk and business risk, they are not immune to market risk. Short-term bonds fluctuate less in price than long-term bonds. Therefore, the 1994 offers greater capital stability than the 2008. This, too, argues in favor of the 1994 bond.

However, there are two reasons why you might prefer the 2008 over the 1994, and the term-yield graph identifies those reasons. First, interest rates can fall, as they do in Figure 11–1, and the shorter bond doesn't lock in a longer yield. The investor who buys the 2008 bond is assured of locking in slightly under nine percent until the next century. The 1994 bond offers this yield only until 1994, at which time reinvestment opportunities might be lower. The longer bond offers longer continuity of yield. Second, if interest rates fall, the longer bond will increase in price. Although capital gains are secondary for our income-centered purposes, they are a potential "extra" from this income investment.

The term-yield graph confirms our intentions as income investors. If we want greater capital stability and greater reinvestment opportunity, we go shorter. If we want longer continuity of yield and will accept upside gains as the companion to downside losses, we go long. The term-yield graph enables us to define "longer" and "shorter" as specific years by reference to the total spectrum of yields.

ASSESSING THE GREATEST YIELD—QUALITY CONSTANT, MARKET RISK INDIFFERENT

Long-term income investors, such as those buying Treasuries for IRAs, might demand the greatest yield but will not forsake any quality and are not concerned about price fluctuations. Figure 11–1 clearly directs those income investors to 2002. Yield and term don't tell us why that year is the year we want, but they certainly identify where it is.

If the yield elbow is in a cast and rates don't differentiate themselves over the whole spectrum of term yields, we follow liquidity preference and stay short.

ASSESSING THE GREATEST YIELD—QUALITY TRADE-OFFS, MATURITY CONSTANT

Some investors want the highest yields and are less concerned about quality. They are not contemptuous of quality, but yields are paramount for them. We still have to ask these aggressive investors a question: "How much quality will you forsake for greater income?" We can't answer this question for such investors, but we address it by referring to the term-yield graph and our discussion of ratings.

Let's say that for a given maturity AAA Treasuries are yielding nine percent, a BBB corporate ten percent, and a CCC corporate 12 percent. On a single bond, par value $1,000, their respective coupon yields will be $90, $100, and $120. The BBB bond pays $10 per bond per year more than the AAA Treasury, and the CCC bond, clearly speculative with greater default risk, pays $30 more than the AAA Treasury and $20 more than the minimum-grade investment-quality bond. Is ten bucks enough to compensate for greater default risk? Is 20? Is 30? Now examine current yield to see what the market's circulation is.

The aggressive investor has to answer, but term-yield shows how to ask the correct questions. Moreover, term-yield helps assess the desirability of other yields, such as yield to maturity versus current yield.

CONSTANT DOLLAR SECURITIES—QUALITY, MARKET RISK, YIELD

Many income investors cannot stand price fluctuations and therefore confine their income investments to untraded, constant dollar securities such as certificates. Capital stability (immunity to market risk) is a considerable advantage, but it is an advantage that requires a sacrifice, and usually that sacrifice is less yield. By comparing the Treasury yields that are available at each maturity with certificate yields at the same maturity, you can determine how much yield you sacrifice for the advantage of capital stability.

Would you accept an 8^1/$_2$ percent yield on a 12-year certificate knowing that Treasuries of the same maturity yield close to ten percent? That yield difference is the "payment" you make for capital stability, and the term-yield graph identifies how much yield you sacrifice for stability.

Another "payment" for capital stability may be forfeiture of liquidity. This is also the case with certificates. Again, we have the same comparison. The certificate yields 8^1/$_2$ percent, the Treasury close to ten percent. To this we add that the certificate is illiquid. Are lower interest plus lower liquidity too dear a price to pay for capital stability? You decide, and the term-yield graph coupled with an understanding of different income securities shows you yield cost of your decision.

COMPARING INVESTMENTS OF HIGHER YIELD

Let's say we have a quality investment—a corporate bond rated AA—that is paying enough interest to compensate for the sacrifice of Treasury bond quality. This is no junk bond; it is acceptable for quality-conscious income investors.

The quality of this bond isn't very different from that of a Treasury, and its yield is sufficient compensation for the difference. With corporate bonds we are not sacrificing liquidity, and the maturities of corporate bonds often coincide with the maturities of Treasuries. We've examined every aspect of this situation, and we've concluded that this bond isn't a bad deal. We may think, however, that the term-yield graph is irrelevant to this choice.

Absolutely not. Our understanding of term-yield and our ability to compare investments have enabled us to make this decision. We arrive at an intelligent decision because we have the knowledge of Section II and term-yield at our disposal.

COMPARISON WITH STOCKS

High-dividend stocks are sometimes more attractive than bonds, and we noted that dividends must be compared with interest from

Treasuries and with interest from bonds of the same corporate issuer. The term-yield graph enables income investors to affix specific figures to these comparisons.

As we learned in Section II, however, the key issues beyond numerical comparison are that interest on Treasury securities is a fixed, semiannual, default-free payment from an issuer immune to business risk, whereas dividends represent default and business risk in payments that occur quarterly and can be raised. Term-yield shows the trade-off in quality and income. You compare your dividend yield with bond yields and decide whether quarterly payments that don't have to be paid but may be increased are preferable.

TERM-YIELD AND DECISIONS TO SELL OR CONSUME

Apart from the many reasons for bailing out that we've identified, income investors sell when a present investment isn't competitive in present markets. This information is obvious from a term-yield graph. You compare the yields of your investment with the yields of the quality investment that are shown on the term-yield graph.

The end of all investment is consumption, and consumption is of two types: consumption of durables, or lasting goods, and consumption of nondurables, goods that have a short half-life, such as food and vacations. In both cases, the cost of these goods is not merely their price but also the "cost" of the yield you could earn by investing instead of consuming and, more significantly, the cost of paying interest rather than receiving it.

When yields on investment are generally "low," cash consumption of both durables and nondurables is more opportune. You are not sacrificing great interest for the satisfaction of consuming a vacation or an expensive night on the town. In particular, you sacrifice less by purchasing lasting goods, such as home improvements or automobiles, because the life of these goods may provide more continuing satisfaction than yields on investment.

However, yield earned is a competitor against interest paid to consume goods on credit. When the cost of borrowing to consume is in excess of income investment yields, it doesn't matter whether investment yields are "high" or "low"—your total cost of consuming is proportionately higher. Your inducement to consume should be less than your inducement to invest, and term-yield reveals the amount of that inducement.

If, for instance, money fund yields hover at around six percent, short-term Treasuries at around seven to eight percent, and long-term Treasuries at around ten percent, "low interest charges of 12.5 percent" for VISA and MasterCard and interest charges of 18–20 percent for personal lines of credit are very expensive indeed. Your interest charges are two or three times as high as money fund yields; if you're paying 18 percent and losing six percent, your true carrying cost is 24 percent. You can figure your true carrying cost if a line of credit is 20 percent when the long bond alternative is ten percent.

YIELD THAT SEEMS TOO GOOD TO BE TRUE

We've seen that income investments establish norms within their types. Through term-yield we identify the pinnacle of quality yields for income investments and the overall economy. When any security offers a yield excessive for its type in comparison with those yields, the reason is greater risk, *regardless of what investment literature protests to the contrary.*

Risks whispered in investment literature but shouted by extravagant yields have been too evident during the middle and late '80s. During that five-year span a few banks, S&Ls, brokerages, bond houses, annuity sponsors, and other intermediaries issued all types of income investments yielding several points above the norms for their types and alarmingly high in comparison to term-yield quality. Many of those intermediaries are now in receivership, and their investors are now paying a painful price for ignoring term-yield comparisons.

There is no reason why these investors should have lost a cent. Term-yield graphs reveal the income truth of economy-wide yields. Responsible institutions don't offer and intelligent income investors don't believe yields that vary excessively from term-yield truth. If term-yield graphs demonstrate that a yield is too good to be true for this time and this place in an investment economy, then it is.

Many, many investors less informed than we have become by reading this chapter continually complain that today's yields are "low." They recall the extraordinary yields of the late '70s, and for some reason they believe that those aberrant rates should be today's rates. Worse, they believe that financial markets are conspiring to deny them those "rightful" yields. Such investors are vulnerable to the high-yield pitches of a few financial institutions. As knowledgeable income investors, we need make no comment on the statements of peer investors and predatory institutions. Term-yield declares everything we have to say on the matter.

SUMMARY

All that we have learned is brought to life through a graph portraying the term structure of interest rates and the yield curve. The term-yield graph enables us to compare the risks, features, and yields of a particular investment with overall yields in the economy as represented at the firmest level of quality, maturity, and yield. With knowledge of term-yield, we can compare individual investments according to each of their specific features. In this way, we can understand what we sacrifice and gain through investment selections and put a specific yield price on our sacrifices and gains. With the term-yield graph, we can recognize irresponsible yields on tawdry income investments and even direct our selling and consumption decisions.

Term-yield puts at our disposal the most significant tool of income investing. As we go forward in Section III, we will also see how the term structure of interest rates and the yield curve enable us to estimate an overall economy and structure our income investments accordingly. We will learn to use term-yield in managing inflation and depression, discover how transient and aggressive income investors rely on term-yield material, discuss the importance of term-yield for retirees, and call on term-yield in creating an efficient frontier portfolio.

12

Income Investments and Inflation

The most mistaken myth about income investments is that inflation devours their usefulness and desirability. As we saw when discussing inflation risk, a fixed payment loses its purchasing power as the general price level increases. Since the end of all investment is consumption, inflation is said to make income securities "certificates of confiscated consumption." For an unmanaged income portfolio, this disparagement might be valid. For income investors who know what inflation is and how to manage their portfolios, inflation presents exceptional opportunities.

In the previous chapter we used term-yield to appraise the features of income investments against economy-wide rates. In this chapter we use term-yield to identify inflationary trends in the economy and to select income investments accordingly. First, we identify what inflation is (not what it's said to be and do), and then we reveal why the conventional wisdom regarding inflation is mistaken, how you can recognize the cycles of inflation, and how you can choose income investments to benefit from inflation.

DEFINING INFLATION—CONSUMPTION *AND* INVESTMENT

The most common definition of inflation is "continuous, sustained increases in the general price level"—not a burst of price increases, not increases in a few prices, but continuous, sustained increases in the general price level. This price-based, consumption-centered generality says nothing about your personal consumption and less than nothing about your personal investments.

Since we personally have rates of inflation that may be greater or less than the "general price level" because region, tastes, position in life, and growing income may raise or lower our personal rate of inflation, consumption-centered generalities about "the" rate of inflation do not apply to us as individual consumers. Such generalities also falter in other ways. Indexes of inflation don't reflect managed consumption, and inflation-priced items may be improved products that represent less of a growing income. Conventional, price-centered definitions of inflation are misdirected when accepted on their own terms and outright mistaken when applied to investments and inflation risk.

You hear how inflation allegedly works against income investments: Invest a dollar in a savings account, and at year-end you will have $1.05; but if the general rate of inflation averages ten percent, you will have lost your nickel and five cents more.

No.

The general rate of inflation may not apply to you. You don't have to spend that nickel. What you spend it on may be a product that has been improved since last year and that represents less of your income this year. And you certainly don't have to keep your dollar in a savings account.

A more appropriate, *investment*-centered definition of inflation is "a sustained, continuous increase in economy-wide yields on income investments." Inflation presents one overwhelming advantage to income investors: It produces higher yields on new and existing securities. In comparison with your personal rate of inflation and managed consumption, inflated economy-wide yields can produce genuine increases in your returns. Inflation has one major disadvantage for income investors: Higher yields depress the prices of existing securities. But if you understand the cycle of inflation, you can diminish capital losses and boost investment yields throughout the inflationary cycle.

INFLATIONARY CYCLES—ONSET, MATURITY, AND DECLINE

An inflationary cycle has three stages, each of which has points of identification that are confirmed by economic data, the financial media, and term-yield.

The onset of an inflating general price level is announced every quarter in the financial press. But for income investors, the surest sign of inflationary expectations is a shortened average maturity on money funds (reported weekly in the financial press). When you see money fund maturities shortening, fund managers are investing for inflation, and when you see money fund yields increasing, inflation is setting in. Inflation matures to a peak that is announced by a negative term-yield with an elbow early in the term of maturity (this will be discussed in a moment). Abating inflation is announced by a shifting term-yield, often a term-yield with two elbows.

At each stage of the inflationary cycle, you can secure higher yields while avoiding the capital losses that inflation creates. You can do this by selecting income investments that are appropriate for each of inflation's three stages.

Income Investments for the Onset of Inflation

During the onset of inflation, money funds are definitely the income investment of choice. Other investments fall in price when inflationary yields increase. Money funds increase your yields and retain capital stability throughout an inflationary cycle, but particularly at its onset, when investors become jittery and their concerns make income investments volatile.

With the onset of inflation, income investors know that their longest bonds will take the greatest beating in price. For active managers of income portfolios, the onset of inflation triggers sales of long bonds. While this is happening, keep your head. If you're holding long bonds for their yield, impending price decreases present new buying opportunities for even higher yields on the same or similar maturities. You can retain your quality bonds, particularly those in IRAs, despite the beating their prices will take. Bonds of lesser quality deserve your concern.

During the onset of inflation, it is not necessary to realign your total portfolio into money funds. Although many experienced income investors go to near-cash at the onset of inflation, others wait for greater evidence of where the term-yield will establish itself before committing capital. However, during the onset of inflation all income investors postpone investing new cash and matured investments in fixed income securities. Roll matured investments and new capital into money funds.

In short, as inflation sets in, shift cash and matured investments to money funds. Let near-term instruments ride. Reevaluate the quality and continuing merits of long maturities. While other investors panic because of approaching inflation, remain in control of your portfolio.

Income Investments for Fully Confirmed Inflation

Within eight months or so after the onset of inflation, confluence of inflationary circumstances will produce the key characteristic of postwar U.S. inflations—*negative* term-yield with the yield elbow quite early in the term structure (see Figure 12–1).

Everything we've learned about consumption, new issues, and investors' responses to changing markets explains why negative term-yield occurs during inflation.

Consumption is a greater rival for capital when there is a sustained increase in consumer prices. Income investments must produce yields that exceed inflation and reward deferred consumption, so new issues of debt must carry higher coupons. Business accepts higher interest (say ten percent) for short-term borrowings because high long-term interest (say nine percent) represents a continuing burden. Personal investors realize that short-term rates increase with inflation, so they want short-term maturities.

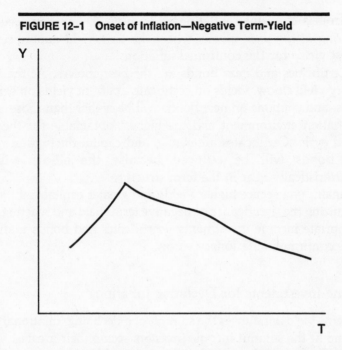

FIGURE 12–1   Onset of Inflation—Negative Term-Yield

As a consequence of inflation and borrowing preferences, a yield elbow is established at a near maturity; as a consequence of economic and investment knowledge, the negative downslope behind the elbow is exaggerated.

Investors know that an inherent tendency of the economy is to establish a positive yield curve, one in which the longest maturities provide the highest yields. During inflation, if long-term yields are to increase and produce a positive yield curve, the prices of long bonds must fall. Price declines on long bonds are a further incentive to prefer short issues, with the exceptions we've noted. Consequently, the focus of borrowing and the focus of personal investing shift to the near term until inflation abates and long bonds, whose price takes a severe beating, produce generous current yields that resummon investors.

Negative term-yield still has surprises in it, but confirmed negative term-yield presents opportunities. For flexibility while facing inflationary uncertainty, keep capital in money funds for stability, continuing market yields and later investment. For current opportunity from a confirmed inflationary term-yield, invest in securities maturing *at the yield elbow,* where the term-yield announces the highest yields for the confirmed inflation.

Certificates and near bonds are the best choices. At the inflationary yield elbow, yields on certificates, current yields on existing bonds, and coupons on new bonds will be higher than those of the preinflation environment and the highest obtainable for the confirmed cycle. Certificates are stable, and capital fluctuation on elbow bonds will be reduced because the elbow will be characteristically near in the term structure.

Again, you secure higher yields and greater capital stability by recognizing the significance of negative term-yield and reacting with appropriate income investments—certificates and bonds maturing at the confirmed inflationary elbow.

Income Investments for Declining Inflation

The term-yield announces the summit of a declining inflationary cycle, and at the summit income investors secure their greatest yields from inflation. Unfortunately, the term-yield announcement of a cresting inflation is not heralded by comets in the sky. To estimate when inflation has matured for its cycle, follow the reports of inflation in the press, monitor the maturities and yields of money funds, and track the term-yield until its behavior reflects inflation information from confirming sources. Those sources are numerous.

Money fund yields begin to decline, and fund maturities lengthen. New bonds brought to market have lower coupons and longer maturities. The prices of existing bonds begin to climb, reducing their current yields. Investors show greater enthusiasm for locking in rates on longer bonds, and their prices also increase as their current yield declines. This economic and market evidence tells you that a positive yield curve is beginning to reassert itself.

You can recognize the effort of positive term-yield to reassert itself by a shift in the yield elbow to a slightly longer maturity and by the creation of a double yield elbow at a further point of maturity, as Figure 12–2 illustrates. Besides information in the financial press, you now have investors' confirmation of potentially abating inflation through the camel-backed term-yield.

FIGURE 12–2   Maturing Inflation—Camel-Backed Term-Yield

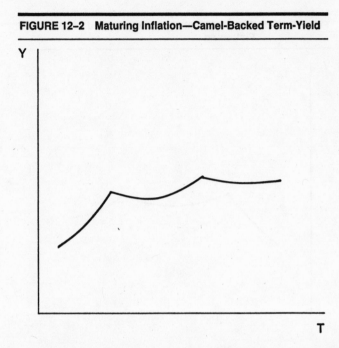

The camel-backed yield curve indicates that other investors have processed the inflation information you've been monitoring and have expressed their expectations in a willingness to accept longer bonds. Remember that term-yield denominates *current yields* and that current yields move inversely to prices. Therefore, the sway between the humps of yield means that yields have decreased because investors have bid up the prices of the bonds between the humps. Maturities beyond the second elbow still generate suspicion; the prices of those maturities have not been bid up, so their yields are representatively high.

The cautious income investor now selects maturities between the yield elbows and no further than the distant elbow, for three reasons.

First, bonds formerly at the apex of inflation will now be closer to expiring, so their current yields will be only slightly more attractive than the yields of money funds. Also, money fund yields will have declined at this stage of inflation. Typically, yields at the distant elbow will approximate yields at the near elbow; however, we

FIGURE 12–3   Matured Inflation—Camel-Backed Yield Flattening

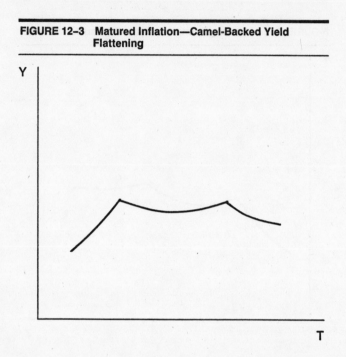

know that the economy is trying to reestablish a positive term-yield, and this prompts us to lock in the distant yield. There is yield inducement to go longer.

Second, investors want to own "inflation saddle" maturities, as witnessed by yield declines and price increases. The desire of investors to buy these maturities reduces their market risk. Reduced market risk is an incentive for you to invest beyond the near elbow.

Third, higher yields at the second elbow indicate that the economy has not wrung out all inflation. Further adjustments in the economy and markets will be necessary before the term-yield reasserts a positive slope, so the cautious investor avoids maturities beyond the distant elbow.

Yields on certificates and bonds maturing at the distant elbow represent an acceptable trade-off of high yields and continuing uncertainty as you cautiously invest during a matured inflation. With evidence, history, and less desirable alternatives facing you, investments at the distant elbow become more reasonable and appealing.

FIGURE 12–4   Matured Inflation—Positive Term-Yield Restored

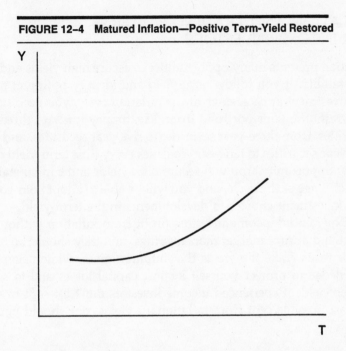

If inflation performs according to historical norms, the yields behind the distant elbow will flatten out, and as earlier maturities come due, the term-yield will reassert the normal positive slope, as evidenced in Figures 12–3 and 12-4. Yields locked in at the distant elbow will reward knowledgeable income investors with gratifying returns.

Admittedly, there have been many "norms" in U.S. inflation since World War II, at least as measured by consumer prices. In their patterns of consumer *price* movements, some inflations have been J-shaped, others have been L-shaped, and some have even been shaped like a W. But income investors concentrate not on consumer price patterns, but on what term-yield reveals about investment maturities and yields. If you do this, even if inflation cycles mature erratically or pop up new patterns, you will have executed investment decisions according to the wisest use of the term-yield and you will have made income investments appropriate to high yield and capital stability.

INFLATION AND TRADING PATTERNS
FOR INCOME INVESTORS

Inflation presents many opportunities to secure high yields and capital stability. If you follow term-yield and identify optimum points for investment at each stage of the inflation cycle, you need not totally reshuffle your portfolio from, say, money funds to three-year securities, from three-year securities to five-year securities, and from five-year securities to ten-year securities every time term-yield offers a new opportunity. You will secure high yields and capital stability at each stage of the cycle, and you will be able to adopt your continuing investment choices to developments in the term-yield.

Experienced income investors profit from inflation without frequent and abrupt market maneuverings, and they should be an example to us. Take the yields that inflation gives, while using your knowledge to protect yourself against capital losses and to secure higher yields. Experienced income investors don't attempt to glean the last possible cent from inflationary yields, nor should you.

INCOME STOCKS AND LOWER-RATED BONDS AS
INFLATIONARY INVESTMENTS

Stocks are often touted as the "best" hedge against inflation because corporate earnings and dividends as a percentage of earnings "keep pace" with inflation. There is now considerable dispute over whether this is so, either in an absolute sense or in an inflation-adjusted sense.

As income investors seeking stock alternatives, we must be aware that an important part of managing inflation is managing maturities. Stocks have no maturity, thereby depriving income investors of an important management tool. Nonetheless, stocks that have seemingly secure dividends and a potential for dividend increases can serve income investors across the range of inflation cycles. It's best, however, to look for dividend stocks in inflation-resistant or inflation-centered industries. Industries whose stock dividends do well during inflation include pharmaceuticals, utilities, and oil companies because the products of these industries are essentials that must be purchased regardless of price and personal income situations.

Inflation may create the illusion of profitability among lower-rated corporations, thereby making their debentures seem more solid. Transitorily during inflation, this appearance may approach reality. But inflation produces business pressures on earnings and debt service, and those pressures are heaviest on companies with extensive debt burdens. Only the most sophisticated income investor ventures into lower-rated securities and the difficulties of inflation simultaneously.

SUMMARY

As an economic fact, inflation may be less ravaging for our personal circumstances than it is said to be for the economy as a whole. Inflation can be managed through consumption choices, and it can be profitable for income investment.

Inflation increases yields on new and existing investments, and by so doing, it presents income investors with opportunities to boost yields and retain them as inflation abates. The chief drawback of inflation is capital losses on specific investments as economy-wide yields increase. But with management of income securities, you can achieve ever-increasing yields while maintaining capital stability.

At the onset of inflation, secure inflating market-level yields and capital stability with money market funds. As negative term-yield confirms inflation, take cycle-high yields with investments that preserve capital stability while reserving capital for later stages in the inflation cycle. As inflation matures and diminishes, shift your focus to the distant elbow of camel-backed term-yield, so that when the economy reasserts a positive yield curve, you will be holding high-yield securities whose rates reward your patience and your knowledge of inflation and income investments.

Income investors are not slaves to the conventional wisdom that unthinkingly disparages income investments during inflation. With knowledge of inflation and of income investments, you can draw increasing yields, retain stability of principal, and profit nicely while less informed investors are blinded to opportunity by what they think they know.

13

Income Investments for Hard Times—Recession and Depression

Recession and depression are the two most serious economic events that an income investor will face, because both can bring an economy and your investments to their very brink—not merely the brink of dismal investment returns, but the brink of an economy-wide abyss.

In U.S. economic history recessions have occurred more often than depressions, and only rarely have two recessions been alike in duration, severity, and profile. Authentic depressions have been much rarer in our history than in that of other nations, although they have been more similar in their characteristics, including their term-yield characteristics.

Income investors cannot manage recession and depression as they can manage inflation, but as always they can tailor investments to economic scenarios, largely through insistence on quality securities. Apart from redirecting portfolios for quality, income investors must deal with recession and depression by knowing exactly what they are (and aren't) and by knowing how to see them coming.

THE INDICATORS OF RECESSION

Commonly, but perhaps prematurely, a recession has been defined as two consecutive downturns in the quarterly measure of gross national product. Although two calendar quarters may be too brief a period to warrant such a damning judgment, the initial but not inevitably continuing characteristics of recessions are indeed a decrease in national production and national income. Income investors look to gross national product as an indicator of approaching recessions, and they also follow leading, coincident, and lagging economic indicators to confirm the approach of recessions.

Leading indicators are indexes of productive and spending measures that presumably lead the overall economy and indicate its momentum and trend. When leading indicators decline over several reporting periods, income investors recognize that there is a greater likelihood of recession. Coincident indicators highlight present economic activity for present indications of recession, and lagging indicators, which trail the overall economy, typically rise as leading and coincident indicators turn recessionarily down. Coincident and lagging indicators confirm the prediction or announcement of recession provided by leading indicators.

For a thorough discussion of economic signals, the economy, and investing during recession, consult *Investing in Uncertain Times*, also published by your author and Longman Financial Services. Although we are concentrating on income investments, many types of growth investments can be appropriate during recession. *Uncertain Times* discusses how to read economic signals to make full use of growth and income investments during recession.

Economic indicators have been accurate in announcing recession, but by the time a recession has been announced, you're in it, and these indicators cannot predict the length and severity of recessions. Recessions may be brief and mild or long and ruinous, and their amplitudes become evident only as an economy deteriorates. This is why recessions are potentially among the worst circumstances that an income investor can face. The first ravages of recession are inflicted on business and business earnings, so income investors facing recession evaluate their corporate securities first.

INCOME INVESTMENTS AND RECESSION—SECTOR ANALYSIS

Recessions are particularly threatening to corporate earnings, and therefore to dividends and debt service. The income investors most immediately affected by recession are those whose income sources are stock dividends, corporate bond interest, and convertible corporates. During recent U.S. recessions, however, selected sectors of the economy have actually prospered while others have languished. Sector analysis identifies *countercyclical industries* that resist or prosper from downturns, promising more assured dividends and interest.

Throughout recent U.S. recessions the stocks and bonds of food, apparel, energy, tobacco, medical, and defense companies have offered continuing stability of dividends and interest. Sector analysis pinpoints the industries and corporations that offer these advantages, which, of course, change from recession to recession.

Sector analysis may also identify geographic regions that resist recession. Corporations and municipalities in the Sun Belt, Silicon Valley, and related pockets of prosperity have, in their turn, shown economy-defying income. More recently these geographic sectors have faded in attractiveness, but "economic Balkanization of America" may again produce regional sectors in which recession-minded income investors will invest for quality.

In addition, certain of our international neighbors may offer similar opportunity for quality securities if they are not sharing U.S. recession, and some income investors export recessionary worries by expatriating capital into stocks, bonds, and certificates of less recessionary countries. Picking another country to invest in may be the ultimate in countercyclical sector decisions.

A broker is the source for identifying countercyclical recession-resistant sectors that are appropriate for the recession in which you're investing. His or her direction, supplemented by the dividend analysis we covered in Chapter 7, will help you avoid the worst effects of recession on corporate stocks—and to improve the quality of your income from a recession-era portfolio.

Further, *sector mutual funds* allow you to concentrate yet diversify portfolios for recession. A relatively new addition to the mutual fund concept, sector funds center on specific industries and firms—the defense fund invests in defense companies, the medical fund in medical companies, the utilities fund in utilities, and so on through 70 industries in which sector funds offer portfolios. When sector analysis has identified promising sectors for recession investments, sector funds enable you to reap the advantages of mutual funds and to concentrate investments in economic sectors that profit from recession.

In judging corporate bonds during recession, continually consult the ongoing reviews of rating agencies for deteriorations in debt coverage. Rating agencies assess the effects of recession on rated corporations. Use their assessments in maintaining portfolio quality and assuredness of interest, adding the corporate bonds that retain investment grade and dropping those that don't.

Certificates of deposit from FDIC and FSLIC institutions are a haven during recession. Such certificates avoid the capital fluctuations associated with any major reversal in an economy, although at the penalty of illiquidity. In a severe recession, however, deteriorating business profits must eventually strain the ability of banks to service certificates.

In short, "conventional" recessions of the recent American economic past have offered income investors profits from sectors of the economy that maintain their earnings and income payments despite an economic downturn. When sectorial opportunities appear, you can shift your corporate investments to these countercyclical sectors or geographic regions, calling on the advice of brokers and the knowledge of dividend and debt analysis that you've acquired from *The Income Investor*. Sector mutual funds also permit you to engage in selected areas of the corporate economy. Aided by rating agencies, you can monitor the quality of corporate bonds, holding those that retain investment grade. In addition, certificates are acceptable, although the presence of guarantors is important.

BEYOND SECTOR ANALYSIS—INFLATIONARY RECESSIONS

Inflationary recession—such as the "stagflation" of the '70s—is characterized by an increase in the general price level, an increase in interest rates, reductions in employment and industrial production, and intermittent decreases in national income. Inflationary recessions are more durable than "downturns," and they present a continuing threat to income investors.

Again, inflationary recession is broadcast in the financial press and confirmed by increases in the general price level, interest rates on money funds, coupons on new issues of bonds, and current yields of existing bonds. You have ample information for detecting inflationary recession and a current recession that is becoming lasting and inflationary.

Even though sector analysis will identify promising industries for investment, an inflationary recession percolates through the economy to reach formerly profitable sectors. Inflationary recession amplifies business risk, market risk, default risk, and economic risk in all corporate investments. During an inflationary recession, avoid corporate securities until the recession abates.

In dealing with inflationary recession, invest in Treasuries and be sensitive to maturities. The easiest course is to select near maturities, five years or so, and be comforted with minimal price fluctuations in bonds free of default and business risk.

But inflationary recessions are long and pervasive. Investors don't know whether to react to inflation or to business recession, and their indecision is reflected in a surprisingly positive (but unstable) yield curve, albeit a curve established at a higher level of interest for each term of maturity, as indicated in Figure 13-1.

The term-yield for inflationary recessions seems to present an obvious choice favoring long Treasuries for higher yields and resistance to business risks. Many income investors follow the obvious and lock in the higher yields of longer maturities. If prices fall and

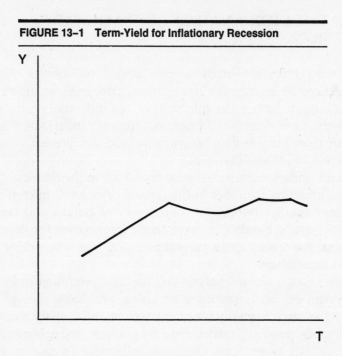

FIGURE 13–1   Term-Yield for Inflationary Recession

yields increase on distant bonds, they buy some more. In short, they take inflation's higher yields and escape recession's business risk through long bonds whose price declines present further investment opportunity. You can too.

But government has the same problem investors have—whether to let markets resolve inflationary recession or to counteract the inflation or the recession of inflationary recession. Governmental decisions affect the yields and prices of quality bonds, so you have another set of concerns to follow.

Responding to Government Actions during Inflationary Recession

Through monetary or fiscal *indifference*, government turns inflationary recession over to the market and says, "Work it out"—as

was done during the stagflation caused by the oil embargo of the
'70s. This governmental nonresponse to recessionary inflation is
identified by unchanging actions of the Federal Reserve (no altera-
tion in the money supply) and by a straight course in federal spending, which is generally unaltered throughout inflationary recession.
Hands-off monetary and fiscal policy is continually announced—
and often criticized—in the press. Identifying a policy of indifference requires no research, and its consequences are unambiguous
for you as an income investor.

Interest rates and default risk increase if inflationary recession is
met with monetary and fiscal indifference. Conservative income investors respond with interest-sensitive short-term liquidity—money
funds and T-bills—for higher yields and capital stability. If you can
tolerate price fluctuations and afford repeated investment, remain
with long bonds, happily increasing your yields and indifferent to
price beatings, knowing that this, too, shall pass.

As a second alternative, government can address the *recessionary* aspect of inflationary recession with loosened monetary policy
(increase in the money supply) and perhaps increased federal spending. Again, the press repeatedly evidences the intention of loosened
monetary policy to reduce overall interest rates, encourage business
investment and recovery, and lubricate the economy so that production will increase and thus mitigate the inflationary imbalance of
money and goods.

If loosened monetary policy is immediately effective, overall interest rates fall and bonds increase in price while retaining
coupons—which is positive for bond investors. However, if there is
hesitation in implementing loosened monetary policy, immediate inflation results from money pumped into the economy. Interest rates
increase with inflation, and bond prices take a hit. Therefore, loosened monetary and fiscal policy prepares you to brace for a burst in
inflation or to embrace the prospect of lower interest rates.

Respond to implementation uncertainties with money funds,
short bonds, and certificates of deposit. Money funds assure capital
stability and higher yields if inflation sets in before the business
stimulus. Short bonds lock in yields if the business stimulus kicks in
before the inflationary stimulus of loosened monetary policy, and
they retain their prices if inflation arrives before the business stimu-

lus. Certificates of deposit can be useful in either case. If inflation arrives first, they retain their prices; if interest rates fall, they lock in the earlier higher yields.

The third governmental policy alternative is to address the *inflation* of inflationary recession. Tight monetary policy (reduced supply of money) and tight fiscal policy (reduced government spending) produce offsetting effects, but in general they take money out of circulation, boost interest rates, encourage investing over consumption, and allow consumer price adjustments to stifle inflation.

Under the inflation-fighting recession scenario, term-yield may present its negative slope, but it is a transitory slope that shifts constantly as tightened policy works through the economy. Use money funds and T-bills until high yields have been established on the term-yield graph.

When term-yield stops shifting and evidence in the press, business earnings, the consumer price index, and investment yields suggest that tight policy is fading, venture back into markets for long-term or short-term yields, calling on a more stable term-yield graph for information. Certificates of deposit will be appropriate *after* the inflation-fighting aspect of recession fighting is over, for they will perpetuate the high yields that were established when inflationary recession was raging. When tight policy is trying to wring inflation out of an inflationary recession, avoid certificates.

Before closing discussion of inflationary recession, it's important to note that it is among the most difficult of economies to manage. Monetary and fiscal policies during stagflation take effect in intricate ways that affect your income investments. *Investing in Uncertain Times* offers a thorough discussion of this particular economy and how you can manage it with income and growth investments.

DEFLATIONARY RECESSIONS

The inconsistency of recessions makes them dangerous for income investors, and one of the least consistent types of recession is the deflationary recession, which is noted for declines in inflation, investment yields, national income, and national output.

Deflationary recession is seductive at its onset because its calling card is declining prices in one or several critical economic sectors—agriculture, minerals, and energy, to pick three sectors whose declining producer prices are now worrying economists.

Although beneficial for the consumer, declining prices may not permit producers to cover their costs of production. Those producers and their lenders, suppliers, and investors receive an abrupt lesson in the economics of loss-minimizing businesses, and the economics of decline spread to the lender's lenders, the supplier's suppliers, the employees and investors of all, and so on. Business, consumer, and investment aspects of deflationary recession are expressed in declining GNP and forecast by economic indicators—this they share with other types of recession.

Any wide-scale deterioration in corporate revenues is a signal to get out of corporate securities. A deflationary recession feeds on itself, and even the bluest of blue chip stocks and bonds can be threatened. At the signs of this economy, you are not overreacting to reduce—if not purge entirely—corporate securities in your portfolio. Even if economic evidence is not compelling, markets will tell you to rid corporates because other investors will be shedding them, and your stocks and bonds will suffer continuing losses. This in itself is reason to evacuate corporate markets.

Municipal securities, as we've noted many times, have held up well in hard times. If you keep municipals in your portfolio, monitor rating agencies constantly. If you are inclined to add municipals to your portfolio during deflationary recession, choose nothing but AAA rated paper, preferably general obligation municipals with backing by insurers.

A deflationary recession is quite simply a failure of the economy to provide itself with the income it needs. Households and the business sector will not be competent to inject the needed income to revive the economy. Only the public sector, government and the Federal Reserve, can muster the income to rectify such an economy. Therefore, your investments depend upon the ability of counter-deflationary actions to sustain the economy.

You must remember that deflationary recession is not so much an investment problem, as was ordinary recession; it is the arrival of wholesale economic risk on a major scale. If there is any attractive possibility in deflationary recession, it is that you can buy income investments at low prices after this economy has passed.

Deflationary Recession—Sector Analysis and Term-Yield

A deflationary recession presents a reverse form of sector analysis: find, not the promising sector, but the suffering sector, and withdraw your investments from it, for deflationary recession also strikes corporate investment first.

Deflationary recession produces a frustratingly unserviceable term-yield curve—at least with respect to maturities (since the term-yield curve represents the highest-quality securities, it will enable you to assess the yield of other securities). However, we generally know that governmental response to deflationary recession is loose monetary policy (increased supply of money and lower interest rates) and increased government spending (either in the suffering sector or overall). That is, government fights a deflationary recession by inflating the economy, encouraging business investment, and stimulating consumer demand.

Accordingly, income securities—Treasuries when business and economic risk are prevalent—of nearly every maturity are appropriate for quality income. But concentrate especially on intermediate Treasuries of seven to ten years. This maturity range is appropriate because it will be the range other investors prefer (which reduces market risk), because these maturities will respond with price increases as government expands the money supply and reduces economy-wide interest rates and because these maturities will not suffer extraordinarily if government overstimulates the economy with inflationary policies to defeat deflation.

Money funds retain capital stability, but in deflationary recession their yields are not rewarding. Certificates may lock in higher yields before the government expands the money supply and reduces interest rates, but extended deflationary recession threatens banks. Corporate issues should usually be avoided in a deflationary recession until the recession sorts itself out. For deflationary recessions, intermediate Treasuries are the wisest income investments.

In sum, the onrush of deflationary recession is usually signaled by persistent declines in producer prices that are eventually expressed in consumer prices and confirmed in declining corporate earnings.

Deflationary recession can be a brief phenomenon, as it is when monetary and fiscal powers act to correct inflation or recession, or a prolonged economy, as we've seen here. The best way to tell the difference is by monitoring economic indicators. In particular, you must distinguish between a true economy-wide deflationary recession and one confined to a sector of the economy. It is relatively easy to avoid sector recession by avoiding investments dependent upon that sector. You need a broader investment perspective when dealing with a true deflationary recession.

Again, you need not be an economist to track recessionary conditions, for the financial media will be replete with statistics and commentary on these circumstances. When, with their help, you recognize what kind of recessionary economy you're looking *at*, this chapter will help you look for the right investments. You won't need anybody's help to recognize a genuine economic depression—our next subject.

GENUINE ECONOMIC DEPRESSION

A genuine depression can be an extension of a deflationary recession, just as it can originate from single- or multiple-sector "depressions" that percolate through an economy to feed on themselves. In international economic history, depressions have appeared as the "correction" of an intensely inflated economy and as the calamitous result of economies abused by legislative, monetary and fiscal, or business and banking policies. Because our economy tends to inflate, not deflate, U.S. depressions often seem to rise up out of nowhere.

A depression is *total* and continuing macroeconomic decline in a *national* economy's business output, business income, employment, personal income, corporate and personal assets, consumer confidence, prices, and virtually any other measurable economic characteristic.

Depressions are further marked by an excess of inventories over consumer demand, a decline in consumer purchasing power even though overall prices have declined, and a vacuum of confidence in all aspects of the economy. Thus, depressions can be identified—once they are upon us—by continuing declines in GNP, increases in unemployment, declines in business profits, reduced personal income, and an unambiguous deterioration in virtually all economic measures, including consumer confidence. Again, all of these characteristics are amply evident in economic indicators and the financial press. You need not be an economist to identify them, as economists will do that for you.

Throughout *The Income Investor* we've seen that we don't have to realign a total portfolio every time the economy changes, but depression is a strong case for exception to that rule. There is no place to hide from depression, so your first investment decision must be to evaluate your portfolio relentlessly for all possible default risk, market risk, and economic risk. Dispose of securities that keep you vulnerable to economic onslaught.

As further exceptions to the standards we've learned, the term-yield graph will not be useful during depression as it was for other investment and economic decisions. Your foremost question will be how long depression lasts, not how long your investments will run. You must also enlarge your thinking about other subjects we've discussed, because depression is extraordinary. The normal comforts of FDIC and FSLIC backing, investment grade ratings, municipal bond insurance may not be so during depression.

There is, however, one thing you can be sure of: during depression you want current income from income investments.

You want cash payments because national income (and probably your personal income) is declining, because the continuation of your wages and salary is uncertain, and because you must preserve your purchasing power if not your outright ability to survive depression. The question is where to invest for income.

Depression and Income Investors

You don't hold corporate investments when an economy and business earnings are deteriorating massively. Often it's argued that blue-chip stocks and bonds are acceptable during genuine depressions. After depression has abated, this is true, as we will see, but when depression hasn't yet descended to its pits, you simply avoid corporate investments. Dividends have to be declared, and bond interest depends on earnings. Unless you are prepared to become a serious analyst of business investments and the depressed economy, these two facts of corporate income investments should be foremost in your decision to purge your portfolio of corporate stocks and bonds and corporate mutual funds.

Certainly, one way to avoid U.S. economic risk is to expatriate capital. Stocks and bonds of foreign corporations, bonds of foreign governments, certificates of foreign banks, and foreign annuities for deferred income can be possibilities if they are issued by countries and corporations that seem immune to a U.S. depression. These instruments may preserve investment income and perhaps provide gains from currency translations—if the economies in which they originate are exempt from U.S. depression. A broker may not be the best adviser on expatriating capital under depression conditions, but you can call on professional and reputable investment advisory publications that deal in international investments. These publications advertise their services and track records, and they are not difficult to find. They will no doubt be even easier to find if a major depression occurs.

Depression will work its way into bank earnings, perhaps representing a threat to certificates and bank solvency. Unlike the situation during the Great Depression, however, there are now guarantors that assure greater confidence in certificates and savings, but there is also some question about how substantial your confidence in those guarantors should be. Guarantors are "obligated" to restore investors' certificates and savings, but not within any stated period. Further, the defaults of banks are typically handled by forcing more solvent banks to accept the clients of closed banks. This procedure requires paperwork time and burdens the assuming bank, perhaps imperiling its ability to survive the same circumstances. There is no evidence that certificates and savings accounts will not be able to weather a possible future depression, but the evidence on their behalf is not uniformly comforting. The alternative is Treasuries.

Money market funds have never been tested in a depression. The exceptionally short-term maturities of money funds, which are broadcast as their foremost advantage, may represent a threat in genuine depression. Being short in maturity, the corporate, bank, and conventional investments of money funds are not merely near to cash; they are also near to the obligation of payment. The nearness of payment can also be nearness to threat of default if corporations and banks cannot muster cash at the maturity of investments within the money funds. They can then reissue their maturing indebtedness, and money funds can accept the reissued debt—a suspect and evasive action called "repapering." The best alternative is the money fund that invests only in Treasury obligations.

Select Treasury Securities for Depression

Municipal bonds brought exceptionally few defaults during the Great Depression, and the presence of insurers may suggest that the same could hold true during another depression. But as should be obvious to everyone this far into *The Income Investor*, low risk of default and low business risk demand Treasuries, bonds funds investing in Treasuries, and perhaps governmental agency debt with a pledge of Treasury assistance during depression. The issue is selecting Treasuries of appropriate maturities.

Knowing what we now know about liquidity and capital stability, our first thought is T-bills for depression. In the Great Depression, however, T-bill yields *went premium*—investors were paying more than par value to receive par value because banks were uninsured and widely insolvent, corporate investments were guaranteed to lose money, and hordes of displaced Americans were, unfairly or not, perceived as a threat to cash lying around any house. It may be highly unlikely that these motivations will again express themselves in negative T-bill yields. Nonetheless, we remember the historical information we have.

During deflationary depression a dollar received tomorrow is "worth more" than a dollar received today. The purpose of investing is consumption, consumption depends on prices and you want a stream of dollars when prices are deflating. In other words, you want coupon-paying Treasuries for their semiannual payments.

Term-Yield and Depression

In some respects, term-yield is not the most significant tool of investment decisions for depression. During depression it is more advisable to select Treasuries with the highest *coupon yields* than to select those with the highest term-yields, because coupon payments are actual cash and current yields are, at least during depression, "merely" current yields.

High coupons are not always prevalent among the most distant maturities. As we discussed, the Treasury sets the coupons of bonds according to the market rates that prevail when the bonds are issued, and this is why Treasuries of similar maturity may carry widely divergent coupons. Therefore, your first step is to pick high-coupon Treasuries wherever in term of maturity you find them.

A further aspect of coupon picking is that other informed investors will also be looking for high coupons. Accordingly, you can expect high-coupon Treasuries to be selling at premiums, and you can expect their premiums to increase as depression persists. Capital gains are the likely result, and these gains can be reinvested to advantage as depression abates.

In addition, monetary and fiscal authorities will be expanding the money supply, increasing spending, and reducing interest rates in an effort to add cash and consumption to the economy. Policy actions will benefit your high coupon Treasuries because their prices will increase as economy-wide interest rates fall.

Shorter maturities of two and three years are not the most useful, as they typically will not offer the attractive coupons you need for depression and their prices will not mirror the demand of astute investors. Intermediate Treasuries of five to seven years will be more attractive on the market. Combined with high-coupon Treasuries of scattered maturities, the short-intermediate range is the most efficient investment frontier for depression.

Demand Treasury quality, seek high-coupon payments, and center on market-favored maturities when aligning your income investments for depression.

Income Investments and "the Devil's Profits"

Quality income investments are critical in surviving depression, and income investments perform far better than rival investments during depression. Income investors are not "get-rich" investors, but depression is such an awful phenomenon to survive that we should know what to do with income investments following depression.

Investors who maintain their financial positions during depression find that when it ends, they can secure "the devil's profits" from investments rising out of the economic ashes. When depressions abate, all kinds of property—stocks, bonds, real estate, and so on— have been so beaten in price that they present unavoidable opportunities for income investors.

We've seen that high-coupon Treasuries and near-intermediate maturities often claim price increases from investors knowledgeable about depression. These investments also profit from governmental policies to reverse inflations, especially expansion of the money supply, commensurate declines in interest rates, and the increases in bond prices that follow. Thus, depression and the countercyclical governmental policies that address it will increase capital for income investors. As depression falters and signs of recovery appear (noted in the financial press through GNP increases, improvements in indicators, increased employment, reductions in inventories, and the revival of corporate earnings) income investors can shift their gains.

The most obvious strategy for profiting from revival from depression is to sell appreciated Treasuries and reinvest in shorter maturities and/or money funds, perhaps even in certificates if the revival seems strong. These are capital-stable investments and havens for protecting gains you've secured. You invested properly during the depression, your quality bonds produced capital gains, and you reinvest those gains in income investments that preserve them after the depression passes.

For a riskier but more lucrative alternative, return to corporate securities. Stocks and bonds will have taken the greatest beating, but the corporations that survived depression will be more solid investments. You can take your gains from Treasuries and lock in continuing current income and greater yields to maturity from discount corporates, further increasing your capital as discounted prices march toward par.

Corporate convertible bonds of the companies that survived the depression are superb for postdepression investing. They pay current income; their prices will have been beaten, thereby presenting higher yields to maturity; the conversion feature presents opportunity to profit from the stock gains common to the postdepression market. Also, former income stocks that lost their dividends may again become so as a revived economy aids corporate earnings and dividends. Mutual funds let you employ professional managers to identify promising investments and further reinvestment opportunities after depression.

SUMMARY

Economic decay won't destroy your income investments now that you know what inflation, recession, and depression mean for income investments and investors.

Income investors confront recession and depression through knowledge of how economies behave, of what income investments are appropriate, and of how governmental policies influence their choices. Insistence on quality investments is foremost during economic hard times, and sector analysis reveals which investments are likely to do well or badly during mild or deep downturns.

Income investors know in particular that business risk is the first casualty of broad economic risk and that corporate securities earn a hard look when economies deteriorate. So do their lenders and the certificates they offer. Term-yield is again a significant tool in assessing inflationary and deflationary recessions, although depression-era investing calls for solid coupons and attention to market-favored maturities in an efficient frontier portfolio for depression.

Income investments can be aligned to endure hard times success-fully, and with informed reading they can be positioned to sustain continuing advantages after conditions correct. Even though reces-sions are erratic in our economy, you can select income investments appropriate to their conditions. Genuine depression also rewards you, because it demands income investments as the correct invest-ment response.

14

The Aggressive or Transient Income Investor

As confirmed income investors, we employ all types of income investments for continuing cash or compounding and we manage risks with income investments bearing reduced exposure to identified risks. Income investments are permanent fixtures in our portfolio. In contrast, transient income investors use short-term income investments as parking lots for capital, relying on short income investments for liquidity, capital stability, and income while waiting to reinvest elsewhere. Aggressive income investors also employ income investments as permanent aspects of their portfolio, but they call on income investments for deliberate vulnerability to higher risks and higher rewards. Aggressive investors deliberately forfeit quality or capital stability in seeking maximized income—but they know they do, and that's what separates aggressive income investors from misguided and greedy investors. Perhaps surprisingly, we occasionally have a great deal in common with transient and aggressive income investors.

THE TRANSIENT INCOME INVESTOR

There is no more apt illustration of the transient income investor at work than the activities of such investors following the October 1987 stock market debacle.

Following the Dow's 500-point collapse and successive days of 100-point rallies and declines, money fund deposits grew at unprecedented rates, T-bill interest fell almost one percent because of the influx of buyers, and coupon interest on oversubscribed auctions of two-year Treasury notes declined nearly a point.

Very clearly, growth investors fled equities and sought near-term, capital-stable, quality income investments providing protection against the risks that coalesced in October—military challenges in the Persian Gulf (political risk), U.S. trade imbalances (economic risk), a possible rise in inflation (inflation risk), the threat of higher interest rates (interest rate risk), the severe stock fluctuations themselves (market risk), and a drop in business profits (business risk). We know that these risks can be managed by selecting quality issues and shorter maturities, and that's exactly how transient income investors used the knowledge we have acquired.

Transient income investors aren't always growth investors looking for a safe house when conditions sour. They also use short-term income investments to hold profits waiting reinvestment. They select income investments that, having read Section II, we can now identify as appropriate: money funds, T-bills, or short bonds. Their "strategy" in mobilizing income investments is simple. They sell their stocks, real estate, paintings, or whatever, and they use the proceeds to make short, liquid, stable income investments.

Therefore, income investors can be more or less "temporarily" or "permanently" transient, for the range of income investments provides instruments of short term, high quality, and high liquidity. Transient and confirmed income investors use the range of income investments to advantage, and so can you when the circumstances require it.

THE AGGRESSIVE INCOME INVESTOR

Aggressive income investors use all the securities we've covered, but what they seek is the investments and terms of maturity that produce the greatest yields—a portfolio deliberately diminished in investment grade quality and sometimes in capital stability. The presiding mentality of aggressive income investors is to seek higher rewards through *recognized* higher risks.

Aggressive income investors are mistakenly regarded as investment wild men who are out to club any point or two higher yield. They are not. They are investors who know that above-average yields mean above-average risks. They seek those risks in order to obtain higher yields, and they know what risks they accept. Intelligent and successful aggressive income investors also restrict their selection to a specific risk. If they willingly accept business risk through a lower-quality security, for example, they will rarely do so when the economy is stagnating, when the security is a foreign issue, or when other risks magnify the business risk they accept. They differ from our kind of income investor because they seek, not to manage risks, but to profit from them by calculated exposure, and there is, as we will see, something we can learn from them.

Their first products of choice are lower-rated bonds—labeled BB to C by rating agencies—and aggressive bond funds. As we know, these bonds present higher coupon or current yields in compensation for higher business risk and default risk. However, more aggressive, lower-rated bonds also possess some comforting characteristics: interest on these bonds is still obligated, and the bonds mature, thereby giving some terminus to their lessened quality.

The most aggressive income investor may select aggressive income stocks. Although higher in dividends than other stocks, aggressive income stocks differ from high-dividend stocks in that the conditions underlying their dividends—business revenues, management commitment, the payout ratio, the demands of regulators—are more suspect. The aggressive investor's high dividends are not quality dividends, but they potentially compensate for the higher business and default risk that the aggressive investor accepts. Aggressive investors undertake the same dividend analysis as we do, but their viewpoint is aggressive.

Aggressive income investors serve an important economic function: They provide a market in which less secure issuers can retail securities, thereby giving those issuers a chance at the brass ring of American capitalism. Every household name of American capitalism was at one time an undercapitalized tinkerer with an idea. The aggressive income investor capitalized such firms when other investors wouldn't.

Aggressive income investors often pursue the higher returns and hoped-for currency gains of foreign investments as possible compensation for greater political risk, and they also engage in the more lucrative but less reserved options transactions.

Longer maturities present greater market risk, but aggressive income investors sometimes select longer maturities for their capital gains potential if the economy-wide interest rate declines. If capital gains don't materialize, at least they have semiannual interest to console them.

Often, aggressive income investors intend to hold aggressive instruments for continuing higher yields. Equally often, they retain them a while, intending to sell them when another aggressive opportunity appears. In either case, aggressive investors want to be in and out of any investment without delay. Liquidity reigns supreme among investors who willingly sacrifice quality.

You won't find sensible aggressive investors victimized by the extravagant yields of questionable securities, because these "investments" require aggressive investors to accept two conditions that they will not tolerate—illiquidity and the absence of market information. Broad public markets, the hallmark of liquidity, also assure continual monitoring of performance. Only the most knowledgeable income investors will—only rarely—select aggressive investments that are traded in private markets.

REINVESTMENT RISK AND QUALITY

A particular conversion of reinvestment risk plagues aggressive investors. Just as an economy often presents changes in overall yields, so too does it often present changes in the overall quality of investments. As was true of the United States in the early '80s, lower-rated bonds and stocks sometimes mushroom in markets and the economy. Higher yields of these issues suit aggressive intentions. But as has been true of the later '80s, higher-quality issues can dominate markets and an economy. These are less appealing to aggressive investors because yields decline with quality. When an economy tilts toward higher-quality issues, aggressive investors lose opportunity for aggressive income. Changes in economy-wide quality inflict a different type of reinvestment risk on the aggressive portfolio.

TERM-YIELD AND AGGRESSIVE OR TRANSIENT INCOME INVESTORS

Transient income investors don't use term-yield, as they rely on money funds and T-bills for their purposes. Except on those occasions when they want income investments for more lasting returns and will use term-yield in their decisions, transient income investors merely pick up the financial pages and check the yields on money funds. In fact, they probably don't even do that.

Aggressive income investors will use the term-yield to gauge whether an aggressive bond is paying enough yield to compensate for the difference in its quality from that of Treasuries. We saw the elements of their decision in Chapter 11. But there is one occasion on which they use the term-yield as the signal to get out of income markets.

In earlier examples the term-yield pictured the inflationary, recessionary, and "normal" economies upon which income investors base decisions. But sometimes, as with the U.S. economy throughout 1986, the term-yield is nearly a horizontal line with no evident yield elbow (see Figure 14-1). This indicates an economy that is more treacherous than any other, and such a term-yield sends aggressive income investors—in fact, all income investors—the reddest of danger signals.

Any undifferentiated yield curve is not sustainable. With an undifferentiated yield curve, business and government have an inducement to borrow long, but personal investors rightly exercise a liquidity preference for avoiding long bonds. Yield has to crack at some maturity where the yield elbow will reassert itself and business or personal investors can agree on yield and maturity in public markets.

While markets are reestablishing a yield elbow, the term-yield will oscillate like a bridge in an earthquake. Price moves will be dramatic and sudden. Yields surge and collapse and recover. No one

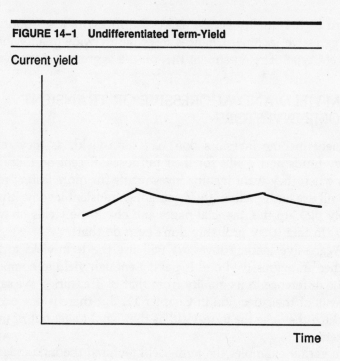

FIGURE 14-1   Undifferentiated Term-Yield

Current yield

Time

can predict where the term-yield will stabilize or where the yield elbow will settle, although it is verifiable that the longest bonds take the worst beating during and after this market turmoil. A flat term-yield is an "opportunity" only for aggressive *gains* investors, because the only prospects for gain are fleeting and are created by dramatic price fluctuations. A flat term-yield presents no information and little opportunity for any income investor.

After markets have reasserted the yield elbow, all income investors will perceive a clearer differentiation in yields. Because bond prices may fall below par, income investors seeking yields to maturity from discount bonds will locate and avoid easily identified maturities. After the term-yield has stabilized, investors can decide whether bonds above par are rewarding for income and once again make income decisions about quality, maturity, and yield. Even aggressive investors have a basis for decision, as we saw in Chapter 11.

But only after the yield elbow has reappeared. In the presence of undifferentiated term-yield, there is no basis for income decisions. This is a time for income investors to be transient and safe in money funds, T-bills, and short-term bonds. For aggressive investors who sacrifice quality for gains, an undifferentiated term-yield based on Treasuries sends only one message: Get out of this market. Thus, term-yield assists in this scenario as it does in more "normal" economic times.

WHAT CONFIRMED INCOME INVESTORS OWE OTHER INCOME INVESTORS

Without the product preferences of transient and aggressive income investors and the market's attempt to meet them, income investors like us wouldn't have "their" securities for occasional use. And certainly our income-investing neighbors teach the rest of us valuable lessons.

At one time or another, all of us will find it wise to be "temporary" transient income investors, and when that time comes, we have "their" money funds and T-bills at our disposal and their example of how to use them.

By the same token, every confirmed income investor may someday be attracted to a startling dividend or coupon. We know what aggressive income investors know when they see that attractive dividend or coupon—never forfeit liquidity, never multiply the risks of one investment, and never forget that a higher potential return means a higher potential risk.

Knowing that transient and aggressive income investors operate at opposite perimeters of quality and often maturity, we can assess our more mediated income portfolio against the extremes of our colleagues. For instance, we now know *why* it's OK to follow a buy and hold bond strategy: Having bought securities for the lasting merit of yield, we need not be intimidated by price fluctuations, because our long bonds are quality bonds. We take the yield that the aggressive investor wants, but not the reduced quality; we take the quality that the transient investor wants, but not the shortened maturity. We know where our portfolio stands in the spectrum because we can compare our portfolios against their perimeters. Our transient and aggressive income colleagues provide standards and understanding that we can employ in our portfolio.

CONFIRMED INCOME INVESTORS AND BOND SWAPS

Bond swaps (also called tax swaps) are a year-end procedure wherein income investors sell bonds beaten in price for the sake of a tax-offsetting capital loss. Then they reinvest immediately in other bonds of similar quality and yield. This maneuver produces a capital loss that is taken against income tax while preserving the yield, quality, and maturity pattern of the bonds sold. Most commonly used with municipals, bond swaps have been used with corporates as well.

You could sell $10,000 par value of your bonds that market forces had beaten down to $8,000, reinvest the $8,000 in similar bonds maturing with a par value of $10,000, take the $2,000 capital loss against income now, and earn that $2,000 back when your newly purchased bonds mature. The $2,000 gain would not be taxed until the newly purchased bonds mature.

As a consequence of tax rate risk in the Internal Revenue Code of 1986 and its continuing revisions, this maneuver could be deadly and costly for you. A proposed tax rule of the Budget Reconciliation Act of 1987 would require you to pay a portion of your $2,000 capital gain *every year*. If this provision is enacted in its present form during 1988, it would apply to bonds swapped after October 13, 1987. Confirmed income investors have been using bond swaps for many years. Before you follow their more experienced lead this year, check with tax and investment counsel.

SUMMARY

Income investments comprise a range of types, and the versatility of these types provides opportunities for using income investments for lasting, temporary, or aggressive purposes in meeting, reducing, and exploring investment risks and rewards. Term-yield information is not very important to transient income investors, but it is used by aggressive income investors to determine whether an aggressive investment compensates for its risks through yield. All income investors obey term-yield by avoiding bond investments the absence of a yield elbow signals that economy-wide yields are undifferentiated.

Quality and maturity, too, are diverse among income investments, and income investors seeking aggressive yields can intentionally accept lower-quality bonds, insecure dividends, and expanded maturities in exchange for higher payments. By the same token, other types of income investors can exclude unsatisfactory quality, choose among maturities, and rely on income investments as stable, interest-earning parking lots for capital.

Of all these alternatives, aggressive income investors seek the alternative of welcoming risks; transient income investors, the alternative of making income investments a means of temporarily shunning other portfolio risks; and confirmed income investors, the alternatives that have been presented repeatedly throughout *The Income Investor.*

15

The Retired Income Investor

As an astute income investor, you have participated in investment vehicles that permit your interest and dividends to compound untaxed, perhaps for decades, while you prepare for retirement. When retirement arrives, it's time to enjoy the fruits of compounded yields by converting your compounded income portfolio to a current income portfolio. When retired investors add employer or union pensions to social security and convert IRAs, annuities, and municipal bonds to pay income rather than compound it, they may be able to enjoy the highest income of their lives. Overwhelmingly, the retirement portfolio is a current income portfolio, albeit one with three special concerns: quality, capital stability, and maximum regular income.

For maximum assurance against default, the income component must feature the highest-quality investments—Treasuries, investment-grade corporate bonds, FSLIC or FDIC certificates, and highly rated municipals. Retirement is no time to be losing money.

Retirees arguably will have many decades in which to ride out capital fluctuations. Regardless, capital stability is more desirable for retired income investors, but the imperative for stability is less than the imperative for income.

Retirees not only need the maximum current income that is consistent with quality; they also need maximum frequency of income. Payment schedules count heavily when you're paying bills with investment income.

Addressing these considerations in your retirement portfolio, whether you retire today or are studying today for when you will retire, requires a series of steps. First, retired investors will be eligible for immediate income from social security, EIPs, and personal annuities. Second, portfolio income must be structured compatibly with other sources of retirement income. Third, retired income investors must reapportion personal portfolios to become income producers rather than income accumulators.

IMMEDIATE RETIREMENT INCOME—SOCIAL SECURITY, EIPS, PERSONAL ANNUITIES

Under 1987 law, retirees may begin receiving reduced social security payments at age 62 or postpone payments until age 65 to receive their full entitlement. The *primacy of early receipts* suggests that retired investors choose social security as soon as possible. By accepting your social security entitlement early, you secure three years of investable or consumable income. Larger payments later probably won't reclaim the advantages of income that could have started earlier.

Most companies give two alternatives for converting tax-deferred accumulations into current income investments upon your retirement: a lump-sum distribution or an annuity. The more advisable is the lump-sum distribution.

If you reinvest your lump-sum distribution in an IRA rollover, you will avoid having to pay current income tax on all of that tax-deferred compounding. You can then invest your distribution in interest and dividend securities that produce income taxable only as you receive it.

Annuity options for EIPs require a joint-and-survivor payment schedule. The annuity will provide lifetime payments for the ex-employee and spouse unless the spouse waives this requirement in writing. Because the annuity contract must pay over a span of two lives, each monthly payment will be less—certainly less than if the employee had taken the lump-sum distribution and reinvested in an IRA rollover. If the spouse waives the survivor option and the ex-employee dies after one or two annuity payments, the spouse receives no further income from the annuity.

Your personal annuity, however, offers more flexible and desirable payment schedules than the annuity alternative in the EIP. Typically, you have these choices with a personal annuity:

- *Lump-sum distribution*—all accrued interest plus principal mailed to the annuitant in a single check.
- *Period certain*—accumulated proceeds distributed over a set period, frequently 120 or 240 months.
- *Lifetime receipts*—the "straight life" annuity pays a certain amount for the life of the annuitant.
- *Joint-and-survivor payments*—the annuity provides income for the life of the annuitant and a survivor of insurable interest.
- *Some combination of the above*—for example, a large lump-sum payment coupled with a period certain or a period certain coupled with lifetime receipts.

In each of these three cases (social security, EIPs, and personal annuities), the longer the period of payment, the lower is the promised amount of each payment. Therefore, in apportioning payments from these immediate sources of retirement income (including the "official" pension plan), it's best to structure them for base-level income payments for retirement. That is to say, payments from these immediate sources of retirement income should be earmarked to cover expected living expenses.

Add up your estimated retirement expenses and compare those expenses with your immediate sources of retirement income. The amounts remaining after fixed and predictable expenses have been covered from your immediate sources of retirement income are discretionary income—yours to spend or invest, as was the case when you drew a salary. With base-level living expenses covered by these sources, your IRA and personal portfolio represent opportunity to expand your retirement income significantly by coordinating their payments with payments from other sources.

CONVERTING YOUR IRA TO CURRENT INCOME

For many years you have been compounding the returns in your IRA or your SERP. Now you need your IRA to pay you, and that means converting your IRA investments into current income investments.

Overall, bonds take precedence over stocks in income-producing IRAs. Interest is an obligation; dividends aren't. Bonds mature; stocks don't. Maturities can be managed near term for capital stability or long term if yields are rewarding. Bonds pay semiannual interest, so six bond issues will provide you with monthly income to coordinate with other payments. If your IRA is with a full-service broker or a bank, certificates of deposit will serve you for these same reasons. Stocks have a retirement income place outside IRAs, but income investments within IRAs are principally debtor-creditor investments.

For reasons now familiar to us, the income investment favored for minimum default risk is Treasuries. However, high-quality corporate bonds are equally acceptable—perhaps more so in a tax sense, as all payments from an IRA are fully taxed and you forfeit the exemption of Treasuries from state tax when they pay you from an IRA. With quality given, income investors address stability and maximum regular payments, and too often they make a mistake: They avoid long-term issues.

Your author will apologize for appearing tactless, but if long-term issues pay higher yields, don't avoid them because your portfolio might outlive you, especially when you can call on the assuredness of Treasuries. Avoiding long bonds is such a frequent error of retired income investors that it must be raised. In retirement, your portfolio supports you, and long-term bonds might provide the higher income that you need to support your retirement.

Long bonds will be less stable, but their income advantages may outweigh their instability. Obviously, retired income investors use the term-yield graph in making decisions about bond maturities, but you can also select bonds for their coupon payments, as coupon income, not price-determined current yields, represents cash payments.

Having chosen mutual funds for retirement accumulations, indirect income investors can retain them for retirement income. Mutual funds are commended by their many advantages, including the advantage of taking all returns cash-in-hand. Remember, however, the indefinite capital fluctuation of bond funds.

The quality and stability of certificates of deposit make them optimum components of retirement portfolios. Although their yields may be less than those of other securities and their illiquidity may be a bit of a problem, certificates are acceptable because of their conservative predictability of income. Some institutions waive illiquidity penalities for retired investors. Again, term-yield assists in decisions to select certificates.

Whether investing within IRAs or for income from your personal portfolio, be attentive to payment schedules. Sources of immediate retirement income will pay you monthly by accord. You must arrange investment income yourself.

INVESTMENT INCOME OUTSIDE THE IRA

Again, most retired income investors call on bonds for income from their personal portfolios. Outside the IRA, bonds bring all the advantages pertaining to bonds inside the IRA.

Retirees become innovative in planning current income from investments in the IRA and in the personal portfolio. They combine semiannual bond payments with monthly interest checks from certificates and dividends from stocks. Retirees enthusiastic about clipping coupons mate government bonds, which pay interest at mid-month, with corporate bonds, which usually pay at the end of the month, and with municipal bonds, which usually pay at the beginning of the month.

When income from other sources plus income from your personal portfolio keeps you in high tax brackets, choose municipal bonds and bond funds for regular current income. Investment-grade quality is paramount, although typically income investors restrain maturities on retirement income municipals for higher reinvestment opportunity, especially if they have locked in long yields within the IRA. Indirect investors select funds with high quality and shorter maturities for monthly checks rather than compounding.

Investors holding Treasuries outside the IRA are better off as direct investors. Distributions from bond funds may be fully taxable, whereas interest from Treasuries is untaxed by state governments; loads by funds may exceed commissions for the purchase of directly held Treasuries; capital fluctuations are indefinite with funds but limited by maturities on direct issues.

The quarterly payments of income stocks and the monthly payments of mutual funds and the opportunity of both income stocks and mutual funds for increased payments might also make them appropriate outside the IRA. As income investments, however, stocks present the disadvantages of declared rather than owed dividends and bonds can be structured to pay monthly income, making their semiannual payments less disadvantaged. Also, dividends are fully taxable, whereas municipal interest isn't. However, directly held stocks may present the income advantages of call options.

Outside the IRA, certificates, T-bills, and money funds provide current income plus the capital stability and market-level returns appropriate for income retirees. Retired income investors can also call on zero coupon bonds for current income.

SERIALIZING ZEROS FOR CURRENT INCOME

Convertible municipal zeros automatically convert to income bonds, and EE savings bonds can be exchanged for coupon-paying HH bonds. Thus, these zero coupon investments become current income investments. But all zeros, whether held in the IRA or outside, become current income investments if you serialize their maturities and take their par as cash payment.

Earlier, we serialized zeros to produce a lump sum at a future date. When structuring zeros for cash payments, we reverse the payment schedule. Instead of investing $10,000 per year to produce a lump sum in ten years, as we did in that example, we invest

$100,000 now to produce a series of payments over ten years. One hundred grand is a lot of money, but it is easily within the amounts that investors may accumulate over a lifetime of income investing through untaxed accounts and personal income portfolios. Here's the schedule of Chapter 6 in reverse:

Serializing Zeros for Current Income

Year	Cost per Zero	Investment	Cash Recieved	Maturity in
1	$870	$ 9,570	$ 11,000	1 year
2	800	9,600	12,000	2
3	735	9,555	13,000	3
4	600	9,600	16,000	4
5	550	9,900	18,000	5
6	490	9,800	20,000	6
7	400	10,000	25,000	7
8	370	9,990	27,000	8
9	350	9,800	28,000	9
10	333	9,990	30,000	10
Investment totals		97,805	$200,000 in ten years	

Here, zeros provide increased income over time—$11,000 in the first year and $30,000 in the tenth. This could be preferable if other retirement payments come early in your retirement. You could invest more in early maturities to receive a steadier stream of equal payments, tilt zero investments to pay a longer income stream, or alter the scheme to accommodate other retirement concerns. But the point remains: Serialized zeros produce cash payments, just as serialized zeros produce future accumulations.

ADDRESSING GROWTH WITH INCOME INVESTMENTS

Given longer life spans and the fixed income nature of most debt-creditor investments, retired income investors must face the need for capital growth in a portfolio. However, growth investments are not the only alternative.

For fixed-income investors, discount bonds from quality issuers provide capital growth. Bond funds can provide capital gains for investors who follow interest rates, as they provide indefinite capital losses for those who don't.

Zero coupon municipal bonds can be used to secure capital growth. Compound accreted value increases yearly with short-term zeros, making them predictable sources of growth even though it comes from interest accumulations rather than capital gains.

By employing the features of income investments, retired investors may not need to invest for capital growth. If income from social security, pensions, converted tax-deferred vehicles, and a portfolio is sufficient and accommodates unexpected expenses, income reinvestment may prove more lucrative than growth investment. Reinvesting temporarily unneeded cash in a money fund or T-bills will provide predictable returns without capital fluctuations, perhaps reducing the need to seek formal growth investments.

SUMMARY

The other side of income investments employed for tax-deferred compounding is converting tax-deferred accumulations into cash income. By coordinating immediate sources of retirement payments with income from IRAs and personal portfolios, retired income investors can secure continual interest and dividends to support a retirement life-style.

Retired income investors consider investment quality, capital stability, and maximum frequency of returns. Of these, quality is the most inviolate consideration, for retired investors can wisely select long maturities for increased interest. In the personal portfolio or the IRA, investors can easily structure investments for current receipts, and they can take advantage of zero coupon bonds, the "no payment" bonds, to produce a steady stream of serialized payments.

If, as a retired income investor, you give proper attention to income investments, you may not need to venture into owner-equity investments for traditional sources of capital growth. Income reinvested in income investments can produce further sources of income through such simple income investments as money funds, T-bills, and certificates. In all that we have learned, it is clear that you can let your money work for you lucratively when you retire.

SECTION

IV

The Efficient Corner Portfolio

Our discussion of income investments is nearly complete. Having covered the general risks of investing, the risks and rewards, and features of income investments, and the employment of those risks, rewards and features using term-yield, we now come to the final act on the income investor's stage—the full portfolio of income investments.

The portfolio we are about to discuss is not like the portfolios of Section III, which covered specific investment situations and economics. Certainly, the lessons of Section III remain applicable, but the portfolios they discuss refer to precise economic, life, or temperamental situations. In Section IV the portfolio is its own referent.

The portfolio we now discuss is a package of securities whose individual characteristics, and market behavior and yields comprise the characteristics and market behavior and yield of the total portfolio. We now examine the total portfolio as if it were *a single security*, and our goal is to produce a portfolio of many securities that satisfies us as completely as any single security we choose. This portfolio is *the* portfolio, not *a* portfolio, and its name is *the efficient corner portfolio*—efficient because as a package the securities it contains efficiently produce the results we desire.

Formal investment analysis presents mathematical tools to identify each of the issues we discuss in Section IV. Having progressed this far in our study of income investments, however, we are conversant with all the basic characteristics and market behaviors of income securities, and there is some question whether mathematical tools can enhance significantly the knowledge we've acquired. In any event, after the math has been cranked out, the conditions we understand will always prevail—time and chance happeneth to all of the formulas we can summon, leaving our knowledge of income investments our foremost tool of portfolio construction anyway. We do not need mathematical tools so much as we need a grid for thinking about our income portfolio, employing the knowledge we've acquired, and illustrating the trade-offs that are necessary to maintain the portfolio we want. The concepts of the efficient portfolio provide that gridwork.

FIGURE S4.1   Variance-Return Matrix

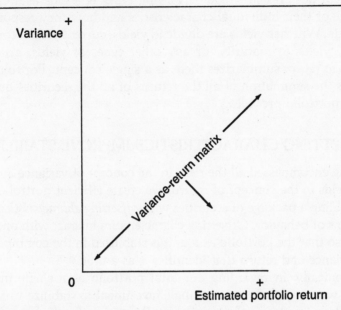

VARIANCE AND RETURN IN THE EFFICIENT PORTFOLIO

To create portfolio efficiency, we must have a construct that draws together the multiple behaviors and rewards of multiple securities. That construct is variance and return.

Differing income investments present differing risks—market risk, default risk, reinvestment risk, and all the others. We have seen that those risks create intermediate concepts in portfolio management, such as capital stability, capital fluctuation, and the relation of yield and quality. In constructing a portfolio of many securities that behaves as a single security, efficiency summarizes all of the risks among individual securities and all of the intermediate concepts into a grand single concept of portfolio risk called *variance—* the summation of all the risks of all types among all packages of securities.

The same is true of yields and the influences on them. Individual securities present single or varying types of yields as a consequence of their individual characteristics and how they respond to markets. Whether yields are dividend yields, current yields, coupon yields, yields to maturity, or any other types of yields, *expected portfolio return* summarizes them as a single concept. Portfolio return is the summation of all the returns of all the securities our income portfolio provides.

OFFSETTING CHARACTERISTICS IMPROVE STABILITY

Having encompassed all the risks in the concept of variance and all the yields in the concept of return, we create efficient portfolios by assembling a package of securities with *offsetting characteristics* and patterns of behavior. Offsetting characteristics interact with one another so that the portfolio as a unit is stabilized in the combination of variance and return that identifies it as a unit.

Ironically, in regarding our total portfolio as a single investment, we cannot rely on any single investment to stabilize variance and return for the portfolio as a unit. Securities of a single type will cement the total portfolio into the singular features, risks, and returns of that type of security. However, by mating securities of differing characteristics, we achieve an efficient combination of securities whose characteristics balance the characteristics of other types of securities and whose behaviors contradict the behaviors of other types of securities.

For example, long bonds fluctuate more in price than short bonds, but their coupons, current yields, or yields to maturity may exceed those of short bonds. Short bonds fluctuate less than long bonds, but their various yields are probably lower than those of long bonds. A portfolio containing only long bonds (a one-security portfolio) will produce one desirable characteristic of an income portfolio—higher returns—but at the cost of another desirable characteristic—restrained variability. The reverse is true of the one-security portfolio containing only short bonds. But if long bonds and short bonds are placed together in proper combinations in a portfolio, the reduced fluctuation of the short bonds will offset the greater fluctuations of the long bonds. The portfolio as a whole will be stabilized at a point of more consistent variability that is rewarded by an average return consistent with variability.

Obviously, this mix-and-match program can be carried into other matings of income investments, but the broad picture remains: By combining investments of offsetting characteristics, we can employ offsetting risks and returns to balance the portfolio's overall and average fluctuations, income, reinvestment opportunity, and performance as if the portfolio were a single investment.

OFFSETTING CHARACTERISTICS IMPROVE RETURNS

From an income investor's viewpoint, the efficient portfolio containing packaged securities of offsetting characteristics will accomplish the most difficult achievement of an income portfolio: consistency of return with balance in capital fluctuation. We have seen that consistent yields are difficult to achieve through the lifetime of a portfolio and that avoiding capital fluctuation is as difficult as achieving consistent yields. The efficient portfolio of offsetting characteristics does not eliminate these difficulties, but it can reduce their effects.

However, the efficient portfolio has greater advantages: It will stabilize returns at a higher level than is possible with a one-security portfolio, while stabilizing variance at a lower level than is possible with a one-security portfolio, and serving our personal preferences as income investors.

To take a straightforward example, assume that we are income investors whose personal preference is absolute intolerance for variance. We might therefore be inclined to center our portfolio on money market funds or certificates of deposit. Money market funds are constant dollar, but their yields vary with market conditions. Certificates are constant dollar, but their yields are established by fiat. If we hold capital stability paramount, mating these two constant dollar investments can serve our preferences for stability, but combining a market yield with a fiat yield can improve our income return if market rates rise or fall. The total portfolio, now behaving as one investment, provides a more efficient combination of variance and return than is possible from a one-security portfolio.

RETURN FOR VARIANCE; VARIANCE FOR RETURN

In creating an efficient portfolio, an investor must, as George A. Christy and John C. Clendenin wrote in *Introduction to Investments*, "measure his resources, present and prospective, weigh the economic conditions he expects to encounter, forecast the behavior of the various investments open to him, and carefully balance return sought against risks to be incurred" (McGraw-Hill, New York; 1974, 6th ed., p. 16).

Christy and Clendenin show us the central issue of portfolio management: determining what variance we will accept for a stated return, or conversely what return we demand for tolerating an anticipated level of variance, in a portfolio as a unit.

As income maximizers examining individual securities, we know that we can be induced to accept higher risk if the opportunity for yield is fetching. As careful income investors, we know that the yields of some individual securities simply cannot induce us to accept the required risks. When we examine individual securities, our risk-yield preferences are fixed at the focus of each individual security.

In the context of the total portfolio, however, we examine not risk but variance, which summarizes all the risks of all packages of investments. We now examine not yield but the return created by all the yields on all packages of investments. And we examine not a focus of risk and yield but a range of risk and yield reflecting all the inducements and disincentives produced by all packages of securities.

THE EFFICIENT FRONTIER PORTFOLIO

Variance, return, inducements, and disincentives cannot be absolutely fixed when we introduce offsetting characteristics into a package of securities, but the inducements we will accept and the disincentives we will avoid can be expressed as a single curve. That

FIGURE S4.2   Efficient Frontier

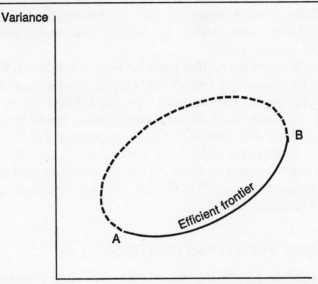

curve is called *the efficient frontier*, and the varying packages of securities contained along points on the frontier are called *efficient
frontier portfolios.*

Our total portfolio options weighted against variance and return are recognized by the ellipse on the variance-return field. The
ellipse reveals the truth that we establish as personal investors creating a portfolio of multiple securities. We will accept higher variance
to achieve some levels of return. Our flexibility is represented along
the solid A–B curve, the efficient frontier portfolios—all packages
of securities whose offsetting risks and differing rewards are acceptable for the variance they require and the returns they may produce
as a total portfolio.

However, when, according to our preferences, portfolio variance becomes intolerable or return insufficient, no inducement of
return will attract us. Therefore, the ellipse retreats upon itself. Beyond the point of retreat, Point B, our portfolio is no longer acceptable to us.

Point A, the zero-variance point, is a combination of investments that features minimal fluctuations but the lowest expected returns. Point A might represent such investments as high-quality, short-maturity, capital-stable, predictable yield certificates, short bonds, or money funds.

Point B offers the highest expected returns but also the highest variance we will accept. Point B might represent a package of investments that produce returns of all types but are also higher in variance of all kinds, such as long bonds, lower-grade bonds, any maturity bonds that bear higher coupons, current yields, yields to maturity, or dividend yields from stocks.

The economy creates Point A through changing market conditions, changing economic conditions, and changing economy-wide yields. We create Point B.

PERSONAL PORTFOLIO PREFERENCES

By centering on ourselves as the arbiters of acceptable variance and acceptable yield, we avoid computations and call on knowledge from Sections I, II, and III. We know the risks and characteristics of income investments and the effects of changing economies on income investments. We are aware of our financial aspirations, preferences, holding or trading patterns, and investment temperament. We may not be able to quantify these particulars precisely, but then neither can the formulas. We bring all the knowledge and resources that Christy and Clendenin describe in establishing our frontier, and we also employ our new knowledge about the efficient frontier.

The efficient frontier encodes the circumstances of risk-return for individual investments, summarizes the risks of individual securities within portfolio variance, summarizes the effects of all investment payments in return, and, as we will see, encompasses economy-wide variables in its changing field. The curvature A–B is not *the* efficient frontier; it is *our* efficient frontier—the combination of securities that constitutes a portfolio of increasing but responsible trade-offs of variability and return as we define them with the knowledge we've acquired.

FIGURE S4.3 Efficient Corner Portfolio

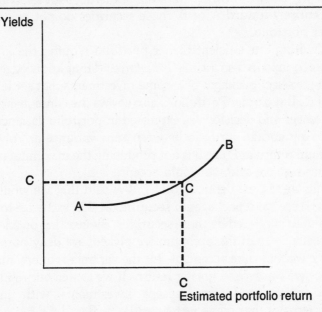

THE EFFICIENT CORNER PORTFOLIO

The efficient frontier can show us the optimum combinations of variance and return to be achieved in portfolios we define as acceptable (Point B), but we know that our tastes, preferences, and expectations may not emphasize the optimum. Therefore, we might select a portfolio of securities with interacting characteristics that stabilize variance and return at a point between A and B along the efficient frontier. The point we've chosen as our preferred combination of variability and return is our *efficient corner portfolio*, and we've noted it as Point C.

The efficient corner portfolio identifies the point at which a security or combinations of securities belong or do not belong in our portfolio. Securities that do not provide the quality, maturity, yield, and market behavior confirming our efficient corner must "leave the portfolio." Obviously, Corner Portfolio C will contain offsetting securities more closely approximating securities at Point A or Point B. But when securities we are thinking of buying shift the corner portfolio entirely toward A or B, those securities do not belong in our corner portfolio.

Creating our efficient corner portfolio requires the knowledge we've acquired in *The Income Investor*, and that knowledge pays off when we select packages of income investments that settle our corner at C. But Corner Portfolio C also shows the consequences of our preferences and decisions as expressed in portfolio variance and return. Any corner portfolio between zero variance at Point A and optimum return at Point B is not producing the maximum return for the variance we said we would accept.

Remember, we defined Point B. We said that we would accept the variance from packages of securities at B in exchange for the potential return offered by those securities. By insisting on a lesser corner portfolio than the optimum we picked, we deny ourselves the returns we said were acceptable for the variance. For any market situation, we can receive greater returns if we loosen our rigid requirements at Point C and accept investments with interactive characteristics that move us toward Point B.

Nonetheless, Point C is our efficient corner portfolio. That may be the end of the matter as far as we are concerned, but economies and markets don't know that.

SHIFTING FRONTIERS

When economies or markets change, the frontier we've picked, the corner portfolio we've picked, and securities in the corner portfolio are no longer stable. Packages of securities and individual securities selected along our earlier frontier display the altered risks and rewards of the new environment in a revised efficient frontier.

For example, if economy-wide interest rates grow abnormally high, as happened during the late '70s, this produces an elevated efficient frontier, A1–B1. In this higher-rate environment, all packages of income securities will produce higher returns but will also display more variance of all types. We know this to be true by surveying the behavior of income investments.

FIGURE S4.4   A–B Frontier and A1–B1 Frontier

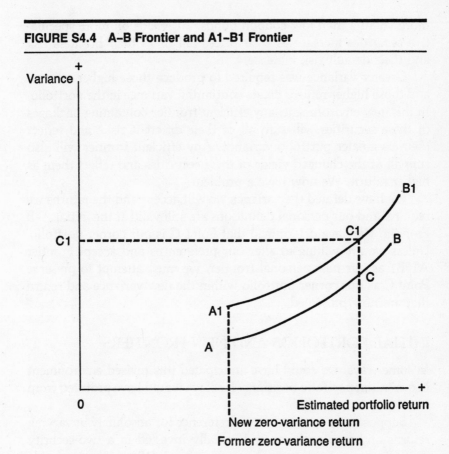

Zero-variance Point A1 is stable at a higher return than Point A. Certificates and money funds, the constant dollar investments creating Point A1, increase in yield in a higher-rate environment, so of course zero variance is at a higher return than the previous zero-variance Point A. Other income yields also increase, but their increase is accomplished by higher variance: Because its price has been beaten down, a discount bond produces a higher current yield and a higher yield to maturity; when prices of secure dividend stocks decline, their dividend yields increase; coupons on new bonds increase, but we have seen that high-coupon bonds are often

more volatile than low-coupon bonds. All yields on more speculative securities increase as their prices fall or as their business risk
and their default risk increase.

Greater variance was required to produce those higher returns,
and those higher returns create continuing variance in the portfolio.
In this new environment, any efficient frontier containing packages
of these securities will sum all of their different risks and reflect
them as greater portfolio variance. Any efficient frontier will also
sum all of the changed yields of these securities and reflect them as
higher return. We now have a problem.

We have defined the variance we will accept and the returns we
require, and our personal definitions are still valid at the initial A–B
Frontier. We have determined that Point C is our corner portfolio.
Unless we are willing to alter our preferences and accept Frontier
A1–B1 as our new personal frontier, we must attempt to preserve
Point C as our corner portfolio within the new variance and return
that are now presented.

INITIAL PORTFOLIOS AND NEW FRONTIERS

In some ways, we could have anticipated this revised environment
in our initial portfolio decisions. If so, we would have profitted from
foresight.

Suppose we had relaxed our preference for absolutely unvarying
returns and zero variance and initially invested in a two-security
portfolio of a certificate and a money fund. When economy-wide
rates increased, our money fund yield would also have increased,
and we would not have been subjected our portfolio to greater variance. This two-security portfolio would provide returns between
Point A and Point C as a result of the shift to the new Frontier, A1–
B1. Because money funds pay market rates, not fiat rates, the new,
higher market rate retains our efficient frontier closer to Corner
Portfolio C.

In passing, we can also note the effect and wisdom of the buy-
and-hold strategy by comparing Point C with Point C1. The buy-
and-hold strategy, as we noted, is appropriate when we are satisfied

with the return securities provide and less concerned about capital fluctuation. Or in a total portfolio context, this strategy is appropriate when portfolio return is acceptable despite portfolio variance. This might be the case, we noted, whether we are investing for current income or for compounded income.

Pictorially, we see the result of our choice. Among the package of securities comprised by Corner Portfolio C, we are content with the return at Point C and are willing to tolerate variance that might result from changing economies or markets. The variance that might result could be represented as the distance between C and C1, but no matter. In our initial portfolio decisions we knowledgeably selected Corner C for its returns, knowing that securities at Corner C might be exposed to higher variance during a changing environment.

REVISED PORTFOLIOS AND NEW ENVIRONMENTS

When we progress beyond initial portfolio decisions and the buy-and-hold strategy to invest new capital, however, we have reason to be less content.

The A–B Frontier represents our accepted variance and return, and the corner portfolio represented by Point C is the combination of securities that accommodates our preferences and intentions. Unfortunately, markets and economies do not preserve Frontier A–B, as we see in the new Frontier, A1–B1. Unless we change our variance-return preferences, the A–B Frontier remains fixed as our standard of variance and return, and our goal is to perpetuate Corner C during subsequent investment. In making new investments, we must reinforce our Corner Portfolio C in an environment represented by new combinations of variance and return, and that might not make us so happy.

Note again the twin frontiers. Note that at each curvature of A1–B1 higher variance is accompanied by higher returns, but variance and returns that exceed the A–B Frontier. All points on the new frontier are above the old frontier—higher variance—and to the right of the old frontier—higher returns.

FIGURE S4.5   Comparison C–C1, C–A1, C–B, C–B1

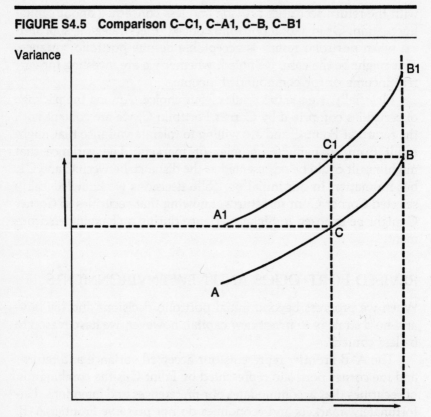

Frontier A1–B1 represents the same packages of securities as Frontier A–B, but it no longer presents the same conditions in variance and return as Frontier A–B. To maintain Corner C when Frontier A1–B1 governs new investment choices, we must decide which is more significant to us—maintaining returns or maintaining variance.

Let's say that we seek to maintain the *returns* provided by Corner Portfolio C when we invest in this new environment. The package of securities producing Corner C returns is now specified at C1, which requires a higher tolerance for *variance*. However, at the level of variance specified at C1, we are not content with the returns provided at C1

To tolerate the variance imposed at C1, we require the higher returns indicated at Point B. But in this new environment the package of securities producing Point B returns imposes even greater variance, Point B1.

If we simply will not tolerate any *variance* beyond Point C, we must locate investments that produce lower variance and add some of the securities in that package to our portfolio. That package is located at Point A1. If we are unflinching in our demand for *return*, we must accept the higher variance located at C1 and the securities represented in that package.

Our variance-return preferences are defined along A–B, and the truth of new economies or markets is defined along A1–B1. We cannot impose our stated variance and return demands simultaneously when investing in the new environment. To do so would require packages of securities not between C and B, but between C and B1. If we draw an imaginary line connecting Point C and Point B1, we will see that the curvature sweeps more sharply upward. Attempts to preserve our initial variance-return preferences in a new environment result in more incremental variance tolerated for less incremental return received.

PERSONAL EFFICIENT CORNER AND MAXIMUM EFFICIENT CORNER

For a present market and economy, considering our resources, evaluation of the risk-reward of individual securities, awareness of how risk-reward are summarized in variance and return, and assessment of future economies and markets, the Corner Portfolio B on Frontier A–B contains interacting securities that stabilize our portfolio at the optimum of variance and return. Our personal preferences may endorse a corner portfolio of lesser variance and return, such as Point C. We therefore structured our portfolio with packages of securities that stabilized the portfolio at Point C, understanding that changing circumstances, such as those represented in Frontier A1–B1, would make it difficult to renew our portfolio at the same variance and return. This we accepted as the consequence of our knowledgeable decisions

---

FIGURE S4.6   A–B and A2–B2

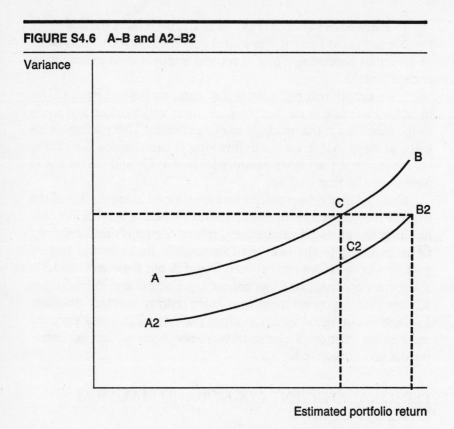

Before we discuss the optimum portfolio at Point B, note that our acceptance of a lower corner portfolio could be more rewarding if the economy or markets reestablish at lower variance and returns, as in Figure S4.6 above.

Here, we see the most positive consequences of Corner Portfolio C. Reestablished economies or markets permit us to retain Corner C, the level of variance we accept, but we can also reinvest for returns at B2. B2 is the optimum corner portfolio of the reduced, new environment, but it is also a corner that permits us to retain our preference in variance while achieving a higher return. Or we can maintain the return we require while reducing variance with the package of securities at Point C2. Certainly, this is the picture of the

FIGURE S4.7   Three Frontiers

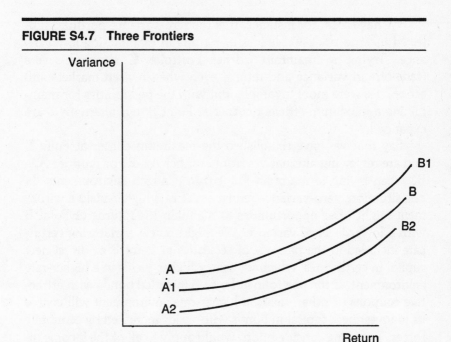

positive aspects of reinvestment risk when we bring new capital to our portfolio.

Despite the satisfaction that a lower corner may provide, in a total portfolio context of the type that Christy and Clendenin describe, there is an inducement to relinquish our preferences for Corner C and strive for Corner B when we initially invest. Consider the variance-return from all of the three frontiers we've seen.

Under any of the conditions that would create Frontier A1–B1 or Frontier A2–B2, an optimum corner portfolio at B, created when we initially construct our portfolio, remains optimum when economies change. If we establish our corner at B, we secure returns that are greater than those of the corner at B2 and we secure returns that require less acceptance of variance when economies or markets present Corner B1. Moreover, in many respects it is easier to maintain the maximum efficient corner than it is to maintain lesser corner portfolios.

We have seen, for instance, that the zero-variance portfolio subjected itself to undesirable loss of returns in maintaining low variance. Trying to maintain Corner Portfolio C required severe
trade-offs in variance and return, even when revised markets and
economies were more favorable. But with the possibilities for maintaining a maximum efficient corner at Point B, our alternatives are
expanded.

Say that we have established the maximum corner at Point B
and are reviewing alternatives from Frontier A1–B1 or Frontier A2–
B2 when trying to maintain Point B in changed environments. In
one situation, zero-variance return at A1 in a higher-yield environment might offer opportunities to maintain the returns of Point B
with a lower level of variance. We might renew a maturing certificate included in the package of securities at Point B or invest new
capital in certificates, which will carry higher yields in a higher-rate
environment. If the portfolio at Point B included bonds with attractive coupons or other yields, a higher-rate environment will enable
us to invest new capital in bonds with yields increased by economic
forces. The same considerations would apply to all of the income investments that we've covered and that could be included in the
package of securities at Point B.

Similarly, a market or economy represented by Frontier A2–B2
can be handled with more versatility if our initial corner was Point
B. Income investments included in Point B, purchased in a higher
variance-return environment, will maintain their payments when
overall rates decline. Some of the variance indicated between B and
B2 will be capital gains if this happens. It will be more difficult to
employ new capital to preserve Point B, but if returns include capital
gains, we will also be reinvesting more portfolio capital. Therefore,
the volume of returns along A2–B2 will be greater even though there
is less of the variance that produces returns.

To phrase the situation more succinctly, a corner portfolio established at Point B can draw on all of the securities packages represented in the Frontier A–B and can also draw on the securities
packages available in Frontier A1–B1 and A2–B2. A less optimum
portfolio, such as Corner C, cannot draw on packages between
Point C and Point B, and revised circumstances further restrict our
ability to retain variance-return, as we've seen when markets or
economy conditions change.

tain variance-return, as we've seen when markets or economy conditions change.

SUMMARY

Having learned to assess individual income securities and recognize how they can be employed under selected economic conditions, we can use our knowledge to create packages of investments that make a portfolio efficient by employing their offsetting characteristics and behaviors. The efficient portfolio is one that behaves as a single unit, and our evaluation of that unit encompasses all of the risks as variance and all of the rewards as returns.

In our initial portfolio we seek to achieve the package of investments whose variance and returns serve our intentions and preferences as investors and call on the knowledge of investment characteristics and behaviors that we've acquired. Although we create our portfolio by anticipating future markets and economies, we are forced to perpetuate our corner portfolio in changing environments, and under the new circumstances we must determine whether variance or return presides in our decisions.

The concept of the efficient frontier portfolio brings all of the basis and intermediate concepts we've learned to their highest levels in a portfolio. It gives us a pictorial representation of our alternatives as income investors, and it also pictures the consequences of our decisions. Apart from giving us a matrix of variance and return, shifts in efficient frontiers illustrate the effects of changing markets on our initial portfolio decisions.

We have learned about risks and rewards, the individual characteristics and behaviors of investments, the influences of economies, and the personal requirements we bring to our investment decisions. The efficient frontier shows what we've learned, how to use what we've learned, the consequences of the decisions we make on the basis of what we've learned, and how to employ what we've learned in changing environments. In short, the efficient frontier is the picture that's worth the thousands of words we've invested in our knowledge.

Conclusion

Since the first financiers created the concept of interest, the first stock started paying dividends, and other securities began making current payments, investors have wanted investments that pay current or compounded income—and for wise reasons, as we have seen throughout *The Income Investor*. The unprecedented array of investments available to us as income investors, their exceptional accessibility and versatility, and their ease of understanding and management make income investments attractive for all seasons of life and for all economic conditions. There is little that you can't accomplish with income investments, and now you are prepared to employ them knowledgeably and profitably.

As we agreed back in the Introduction, most of us started our financial lives as income investors and remain income investors today. We now have the knowledge to employ income investments professionally and more comprehensively, and the tremendous opportunities we've witnessed in income investments will impel us to use that knowledge profitably. We don't need any further inducement to make use of what we've learned, but we have one: The Internal Revenue Code of 1986 (IRC 86).

IRC 86 AND INCOME INVESTMENTS

IRC 86 makes income investments more desirable because it enforces the purpose of investment as *producing investment income*, not producing offsets to income.

IRC 86 nearly killed the income offsets of limited partnerships and imposed new ceilings on deductions and "excess losses" of personal rental property. In 1988 only 40 percent of losses in tax shelters is deductible. The dividend exclusion has been eliminated. Capital gains are taxed at personal rates. Compliance and enforcement are more straightforward with regard to investments than they've been in decades. IRC 86 encourages investments that produce visible current income, and that means current receipts from investments that produce income.

More particularly, IRC 86 encourages you to invest in municipal bonds for investment income that retains consistency of tax treatment, is for the most part not taxed at income rates, and is the only coupon alternative to tax-damaged investments such as limited partnerships.

If you've been investing for your children in a Uniform Gifts to Minors Account, IRC 86 will probably tax their investment income at *your* personal rates. Municipal bonds and bond funds are appropriate to escape the higher taxation of UGMAs.

If your IRA is no longer deductible as an investment, it is no longer an advisable investment. Substitute municipal bonds and municipal zeros that still provide federally untaxed compounding.

Now that the dividend exclusion is gone, corporate bond interest can replace dividend income. Bond interest is more predictable than dividends and no longer suffers a tax disadvantage. Municipal bond interest is more attractive as a substitute for capital gains investments, now taxed as current income, suggesting that municipals may provide higher posttax returns than capital gains. Municipals can also replace limited partnerships now that the offsets of limited partnerships have been reduced and their income is taxable at personal rates.

In addition, IRC 86 encourages you to take distributions from mutual funds as cash-in-hand payments because it taxes interest, dividends, and capital gains as income from funds even though you have not received them. You may as well accept the payments if you're going to be taxed on them. But reinvest your distributions from a municipal money market fund or a municipal bond fund for compounding. These funds promise the best sources of federally untaxed receipts by virtue of historical precedent, and by virtue of the Constitution, which would have to be amended to make interest from all municipal investments federally taxable.

Income investors who prefer certificates of deposit have a friend in IRC 86, for it permits you to deduct losses from investments in failed banks. In contrast, income investors who want tax-deferred compounding have many cautions to consider. Thus far, tax-deferred vehicles such as annuities and investment-insurance products have received consistent tax—that is, untaxed—treatment. But Congress has declared an intention to examine them in 1989.

If you fear that tax-deferred vehicles will be taxed, one alternative is savings bonds. So far, savings bonds have received the most consistent historical treatment in that they can compound federally untaxed (or taxable yearly if you wish). Savings bonds are available in denominations that rival the amounts you might invest in annuities or insurance, and they seem more likely to preserve their tax-deferred compounding than do other products.

Another alternative is self-employment. IRC 86 favors self-employment in many income tax respects, but in an investment tax respect self-employed persons are eligible for Self Employed Retirement Plans (formerly Keogh plans), which feature full deductibility of contributions and tax-deferred compounding. You might want to invest in yourself and a personal business. It should be noted that SERPs have received more consistent tax treatment than IRAs.

As we see, IRC 86 promotes income investments through its treatment of visible income and as alternatives to investments impeded by tax reform. But this is not the end of the matter.

AN UNPLEASANT LOOK INTO FUTURE TAX CODES

IRC 86 is a revenue-generating tax code that was legislated at a time when Congress said that higher future revenues must be generated from the tax code. IRC 86 establishes the direction that Congress can take to procure those revenues through personal and investment taxation. Every informed expectation is that Congress will pursue the precedents of IRC 86 by expanding income and investment taxation in directions already under way. Income investments could become more advisable if Son of IRC 86 Part II, Part III, and Part IV succeed as tax laws, but we will have to wait and see.

But while we are waiting, we had better listen to the farsighted consensus that suspects and fears that Congress will "logically" extend IRC 86 for more revenues by *imposing taxes on income and investments that don't produce income with which to pay taxes.* If this happens, your imperative to be an income investor will be nearly absolute in response to income tax *and* investment tax.

Many observers fear that Congress will declare noncash income as personal and taxable income, as it has been intimating it will for years. For a long time Congress has suggested taxing employer-sponsored insurance, benefits, and perquisites as personal income even though they produce no personal payments and sometimes no cash payments. More recently, emergency food, clothing, shelter, and medical assistance provided as disaster relief have been suggested as income subject to personal taxation.

Unfairly, if your employer's gift of a Christmas turkey becomes taxable income, the IRS will not accept the turkey in payment of taxes. This and other noncash personal income do not produce income with which to pay taxes. Therefore, your salary or portfolio will have to bear taxes on noncash income. Income investments may become necessary to pay those taxes.

A more sinister possibility is that Congress may declare investment income taxable *as it accrues*, not when it is received. As we noted, this is already the case with some investments, so precedents are in place. An expanded accrual tax is not an outlandish possibility, especially for a government that is seeking more money and is currently discussing alignments of economic policies with international trading partners, many of which tax gains as they accrue and tax personal possessions that have increased in value. If investments are taxed on an accrual basis, investments paying current income are preferable on their income merits.

INCOME INVESTMENTS AND SEVERE TAX CHANGES

Should investment accrual tax materialize on a wider scale, capital gains will be taxable as they happen, not when you sell the securities that produce them. Moreover, not only could appreciation on stocks and bonds be taxed yearly, but perhaps also capital gains on property, homes, and investment objects (gold, silver, art). Capital gains produce no income with which to pay investment taxes. Unless you sell these investments each year to pay their taxes, salary or income investments would have to pay accrual taxes.

The most severe assault could come if Congress taxes unreceived—and currently untaxed—compounding in personal annuities, employer investment plans, and related investments. Again we note that these investments produce no current cash income with which to pay taxes, so other income elements of the portfolio must. Now we remind ourselves of the "miracle of compounding," but this time to note that the tax burden continuously compounds as reinvested income compounds while producing no cash to pay the taxes.

As an income investor, you can respond to these assaults if they occur, because possibilities emerging from IRC 86 also favor income investments.

If personal tax rates increase, as seems highly likely, and if investment income remains taxable as personal income, as also seems likely, municipals will produce greater post-tax returns. Municipals have in their favor federally untaxed interest, which has received more consistent historical tax treatment.

Remember corporate convertible bonds as alternatives to common stocks. At least convertibles pay current income with which to pay taxes, and they can be converted to the equities they represent. They might—might—escape congressional attention if more unpleasant legislation applies specifically to stocks.

If Congress taxes unreceived appreciation on capital assets in the future, money market funds (particularly municipals), certificates of deposit, and other constant dollar investments will produce current taxable income, but because they are constant dollar investments, they will not produce taxable capital gains. These old standbys may become the best investments if Congress alters investment taxation.

If accretion in currently tax-deferred investments becomes taxable, don't forget savings bonds as tax-deferred investments. Their accretion has long been eligible for deferral of federal taxes, and the consistency of their tax treatment may survive future changes.

The same is true of zero coupon municipals. They have historically consistent tax treatment in their favor, and they may escape the revisions that threaten other tax-deferred investments. If so, they may supplant annuities, insurance-investment products, and EIPs as they already supplant IRAs for investors who can't deduct contributions.

SUMMARY

We have arrived at the end of our book, but we've only started our future as professional income investors. Investments that provide current and compounded income can also provide a host of other investment advantages. We've learned how to examine the features of the many types of income investments that we're now familiar with, to assess their risks, to manage their individual contributions to our portfolios, and to select the combination of advantages and payments that will best serve our intentions.

Through our understanding of the term structure of interest rates, we can now select intelligently among maturities and affix specific yield costs to our investment and consumption decisions. We have learned how to manage income investments for changing economies and how to employ them in preparing for retirement and in enjoying a lucrative retirement.

The efficient portfolio enables us to stabilize the portfolio effects of capital fluctuation and to achieve one of the most difficult investment objectives—yield and fluctuation that are consistent on a portfolio basis.

As we go forward in our practice of income investing, we see that the 1986 tax law encourages income investments, and we are prepared to deal with possible evolutions in tax laws, even some of the more unsavory possibilities, as income investors.

We are income investors, and the circumstances are in place for us to progress as income investors. The potential and the profit in income investing are ours to enjoy. Therefore, your author and your publisher welcome you as comprehensive income-investing colleagues and wish you the best future that your knowledge of income investments deserves.

Index

V–Z

About the Author

Donald R. Nichols is a highly published financial writer, lecturer, and bond consultant who specializes in income investments for corporate, personal, and pension portfolios. Author of three previous books on personal investing, he is managing partner of Mardon Investment Services Corporation, which develops innovative income investments, including no-interest mortgages, default-free zero coupon refinancings, split investment mutual funds, no-loss commodity pools, and commodity bonds. He has earned recognition from the Secretary of the Treasury for his counsel during national savings bond campaigns, holds master's degrees in english, economics, financial journalism, and expository writing, and teaches economics at Elmhurst College near Chicago. *The Income Investor* is his first in a four-book series to be published by Longman.